FRIENDLY FOX

COLORING BOOK

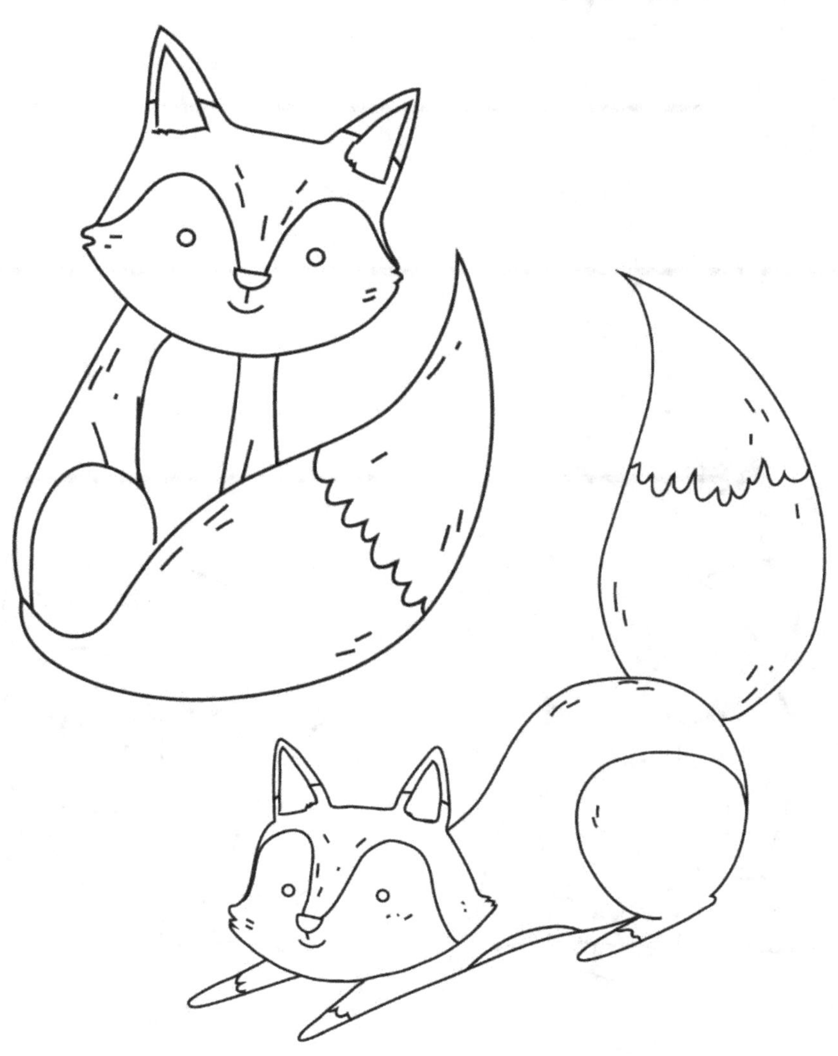

This Book Belongs To

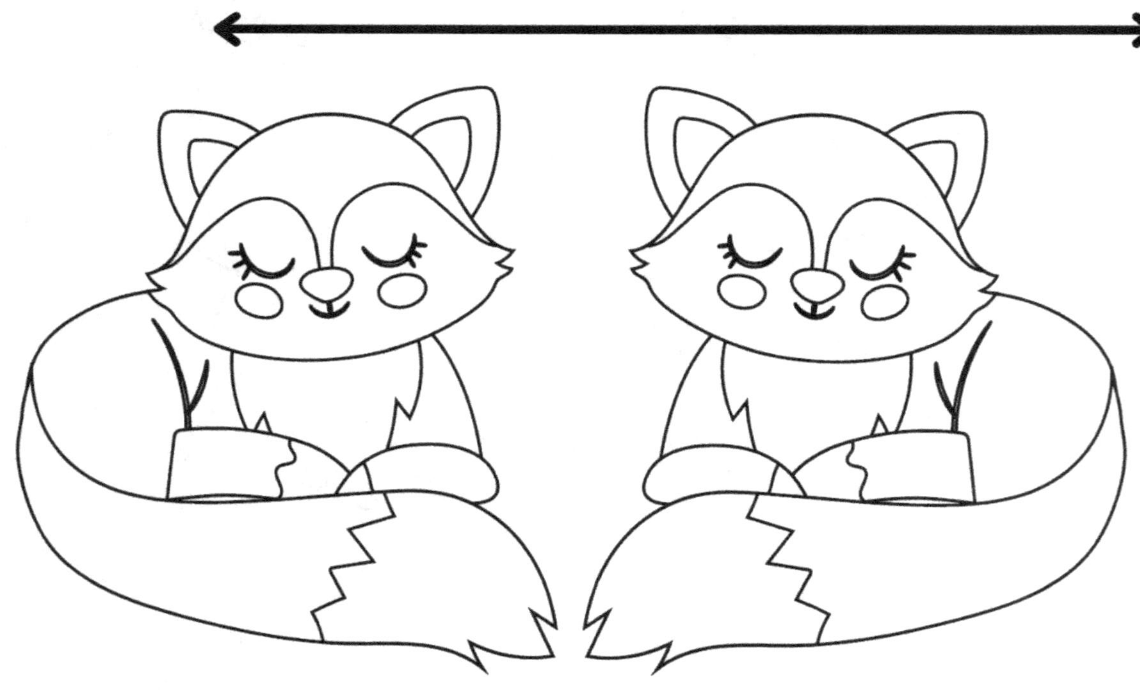

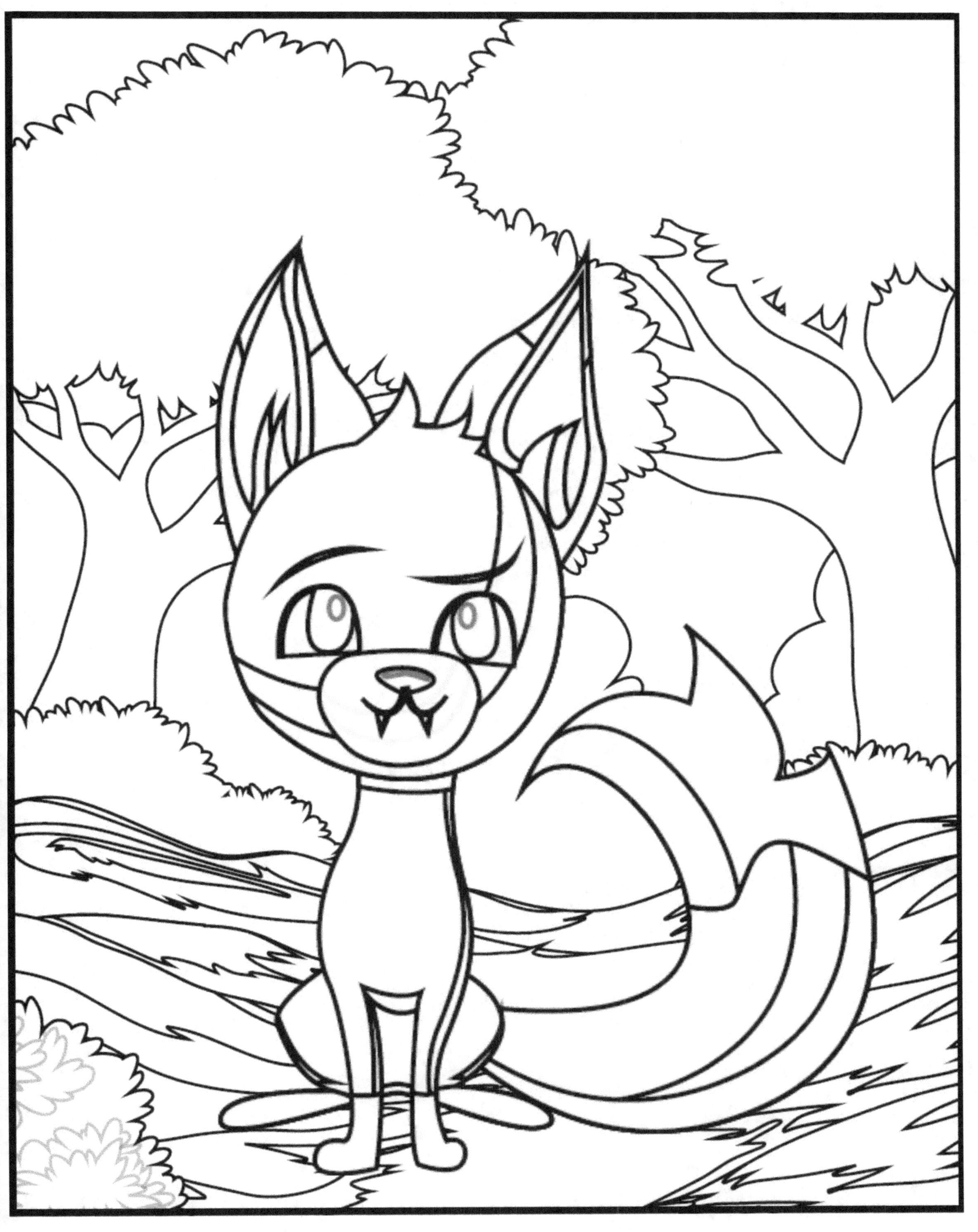

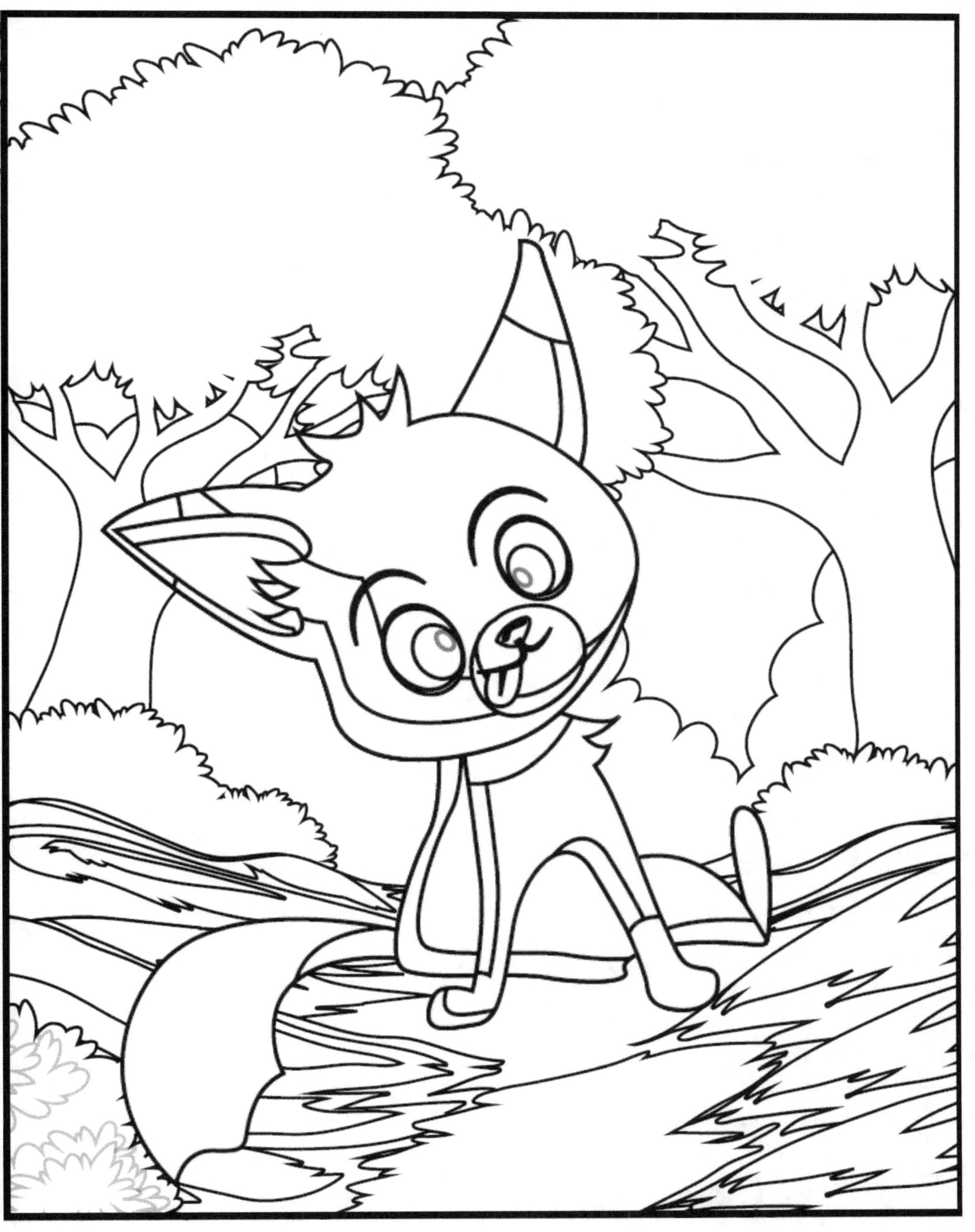

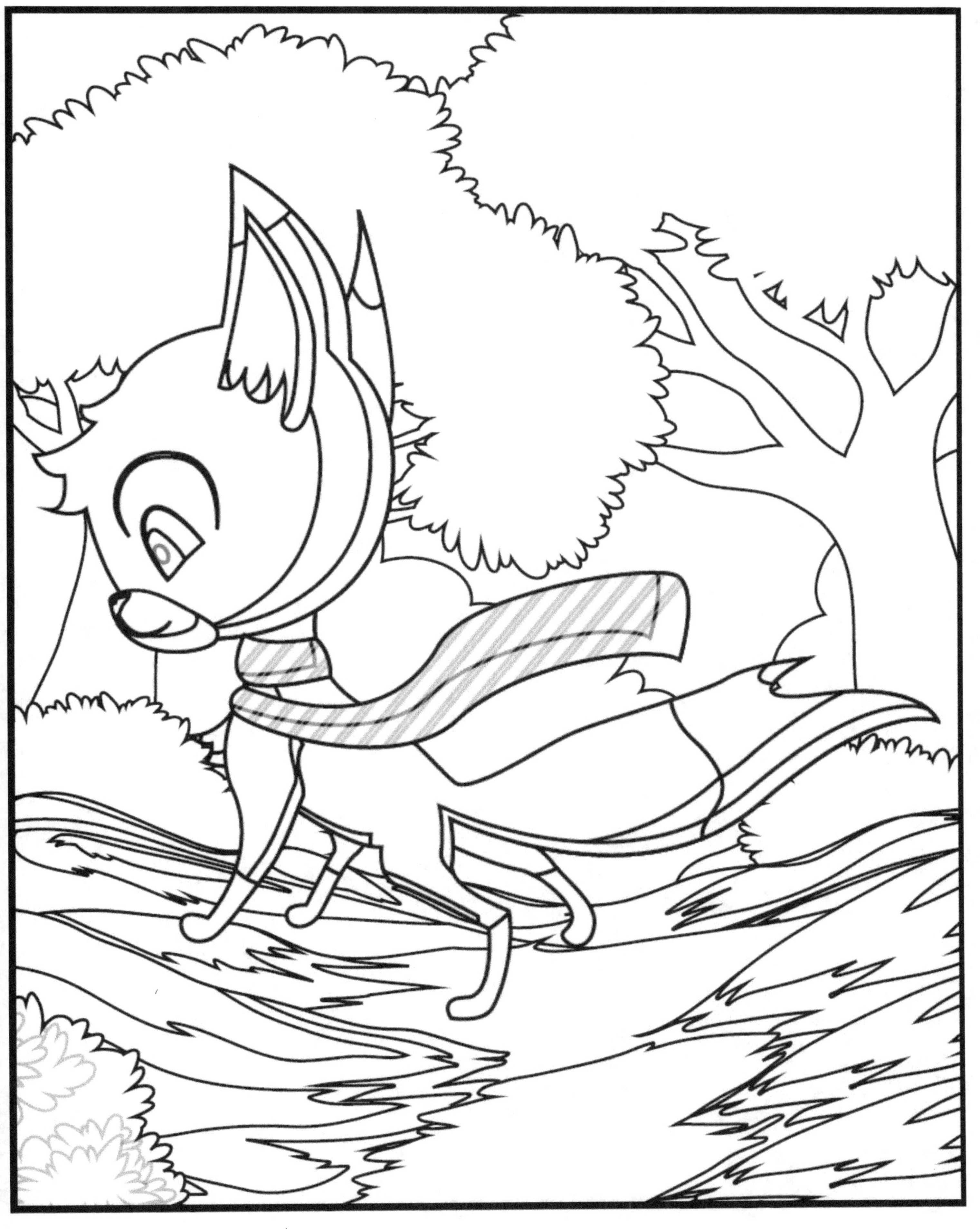

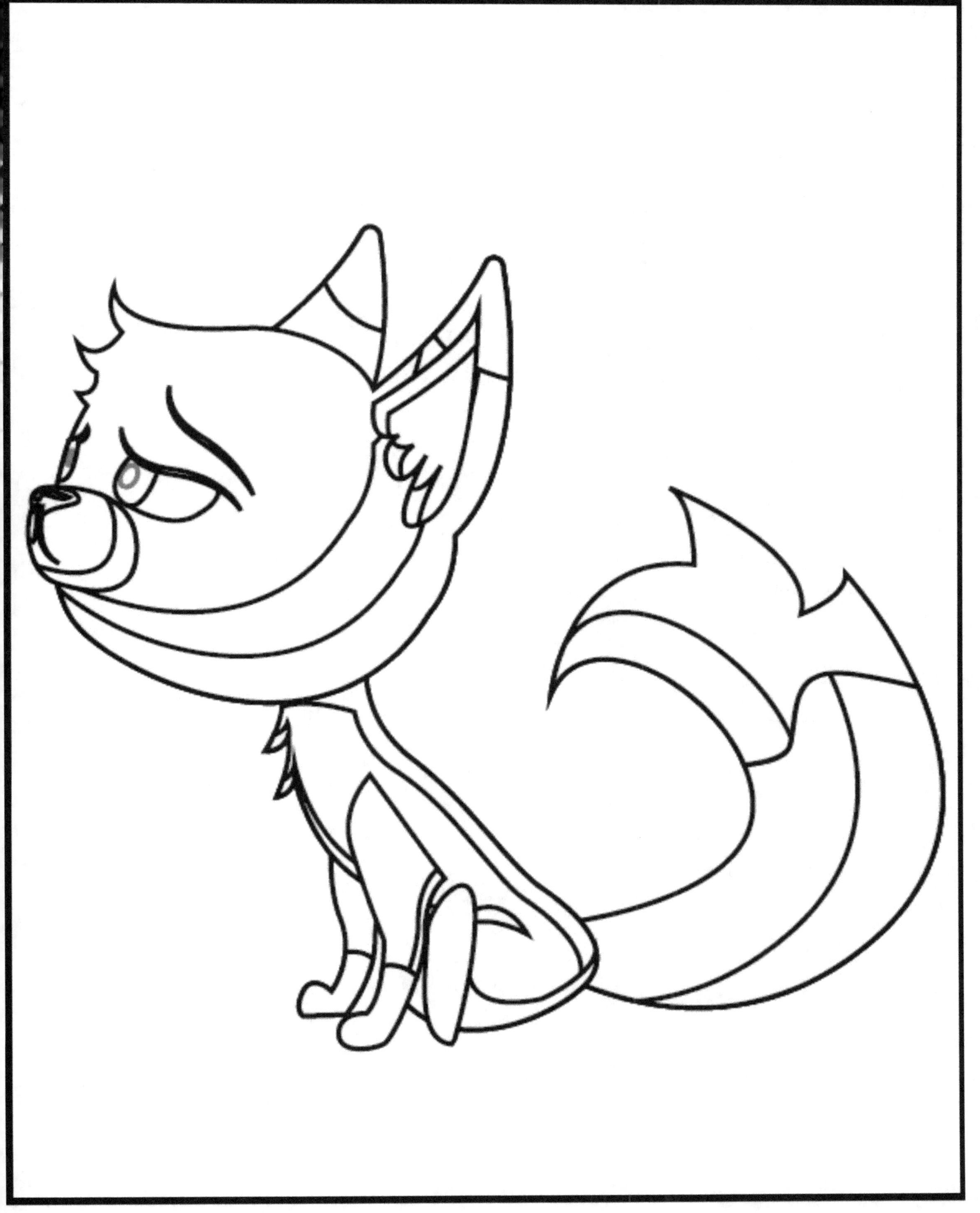

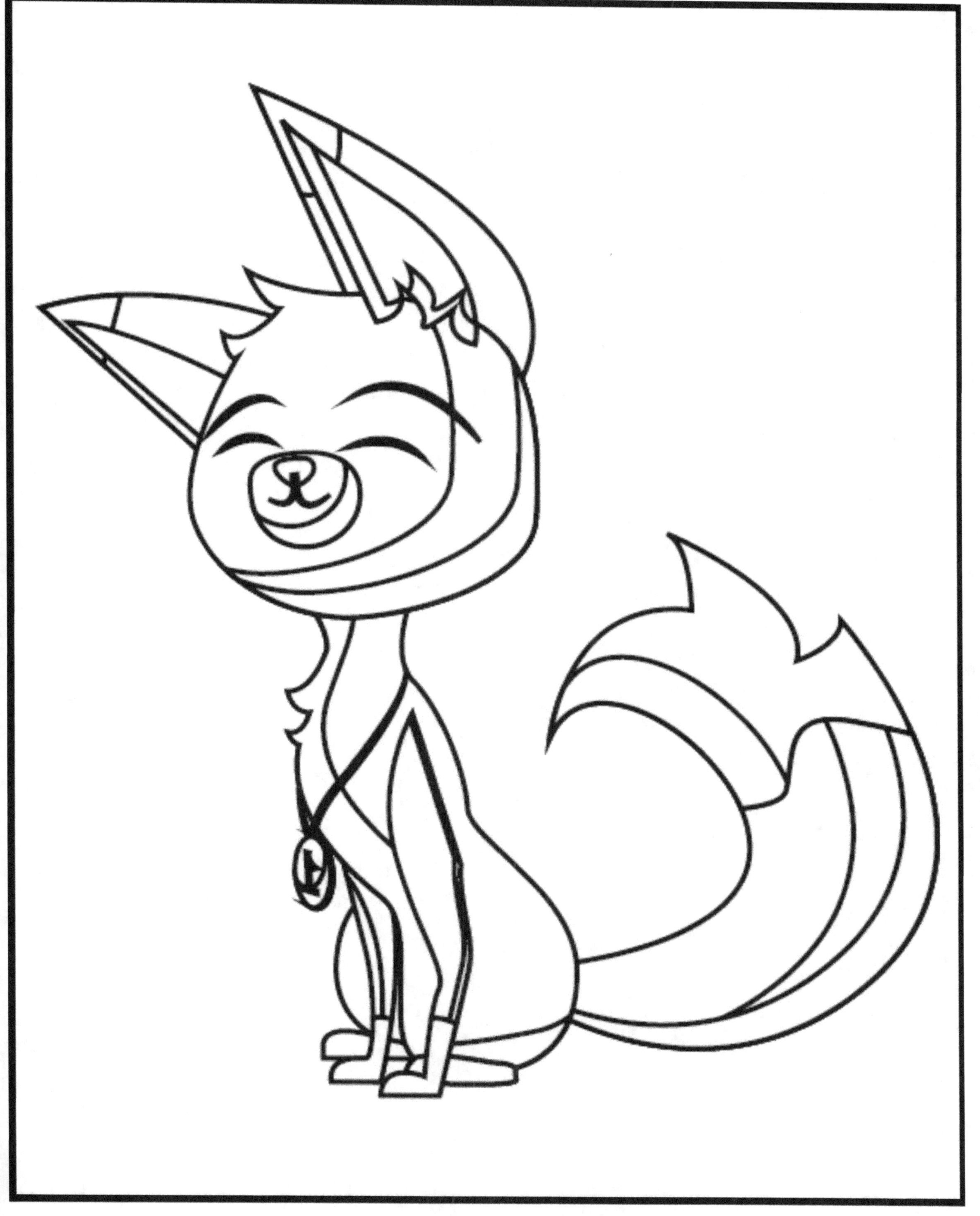

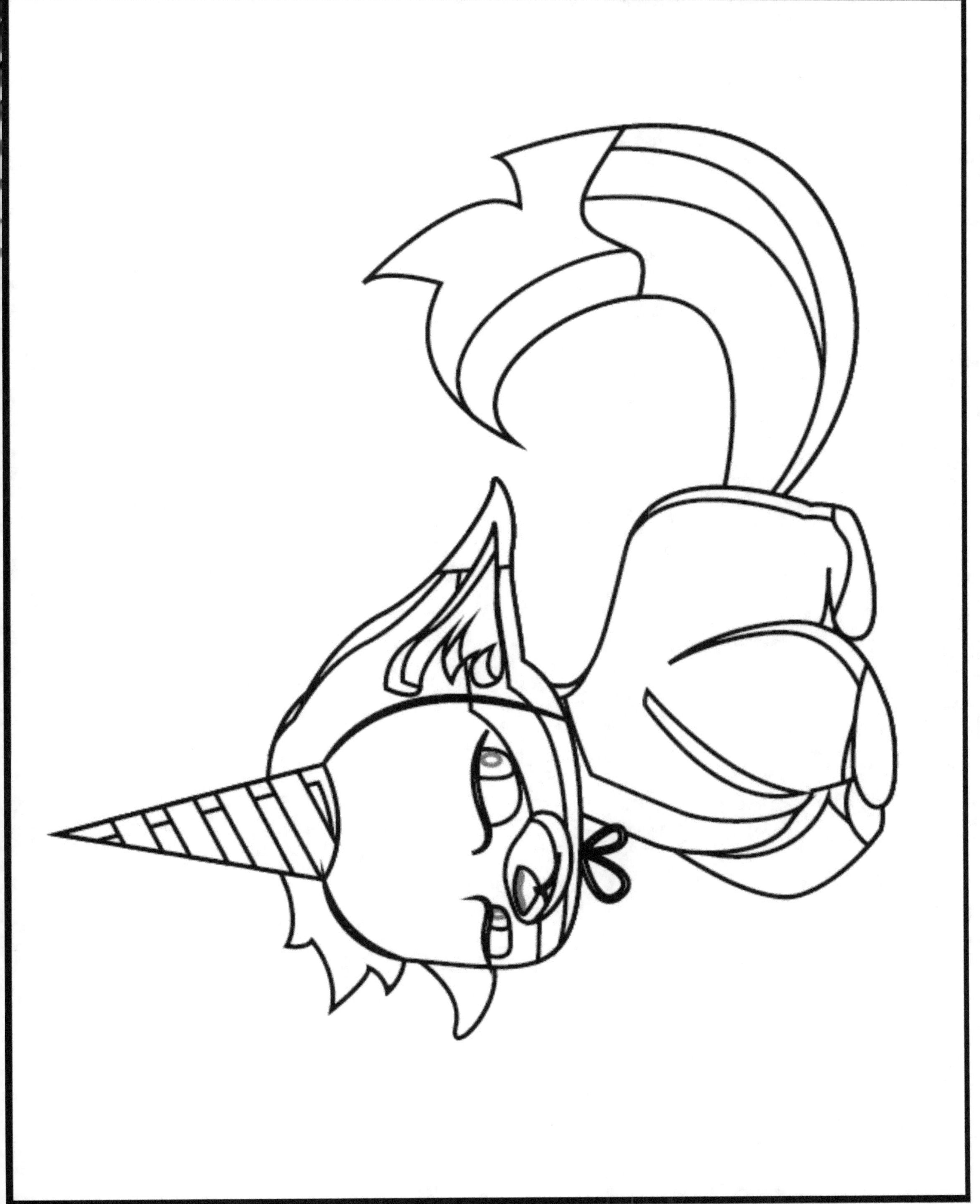

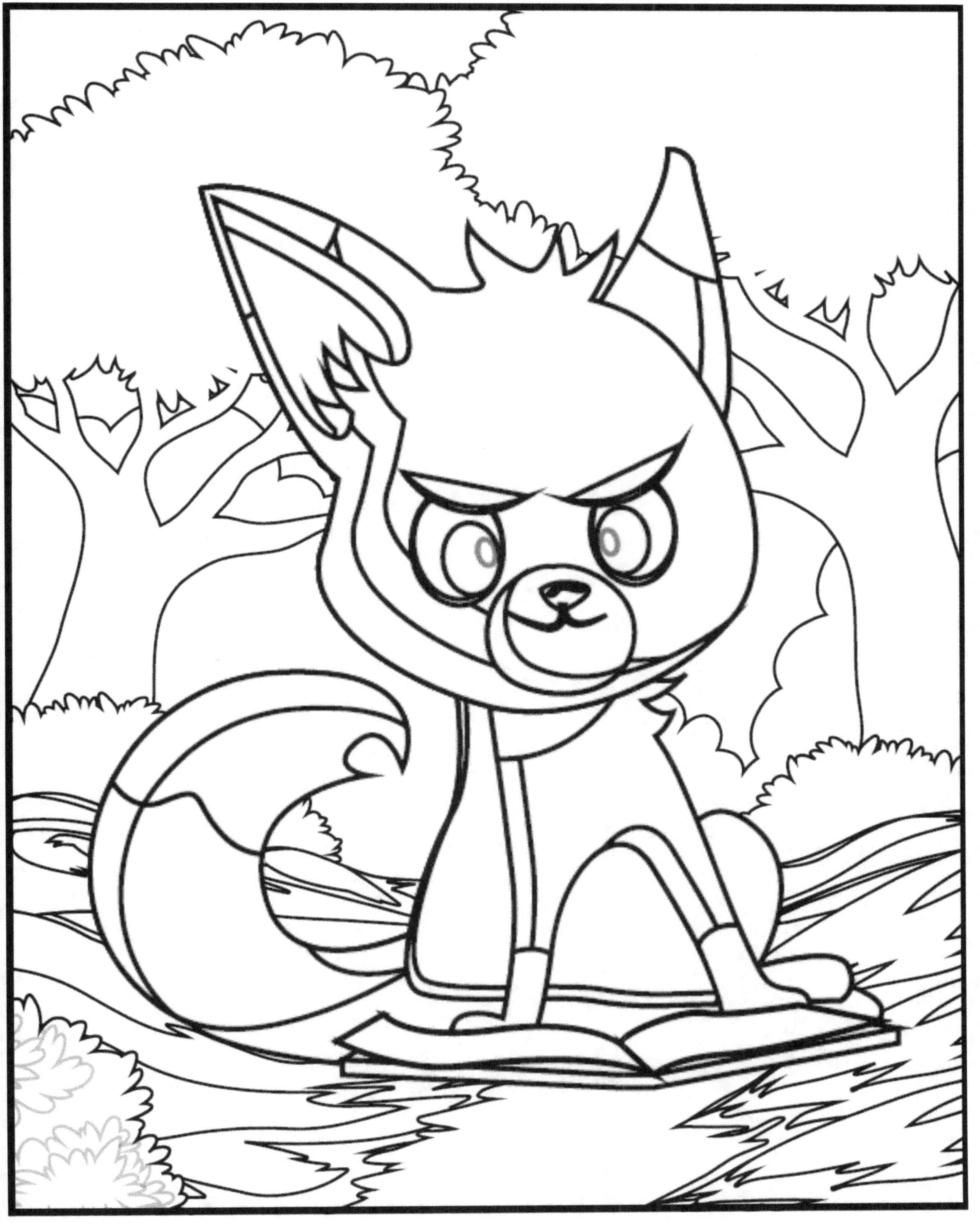

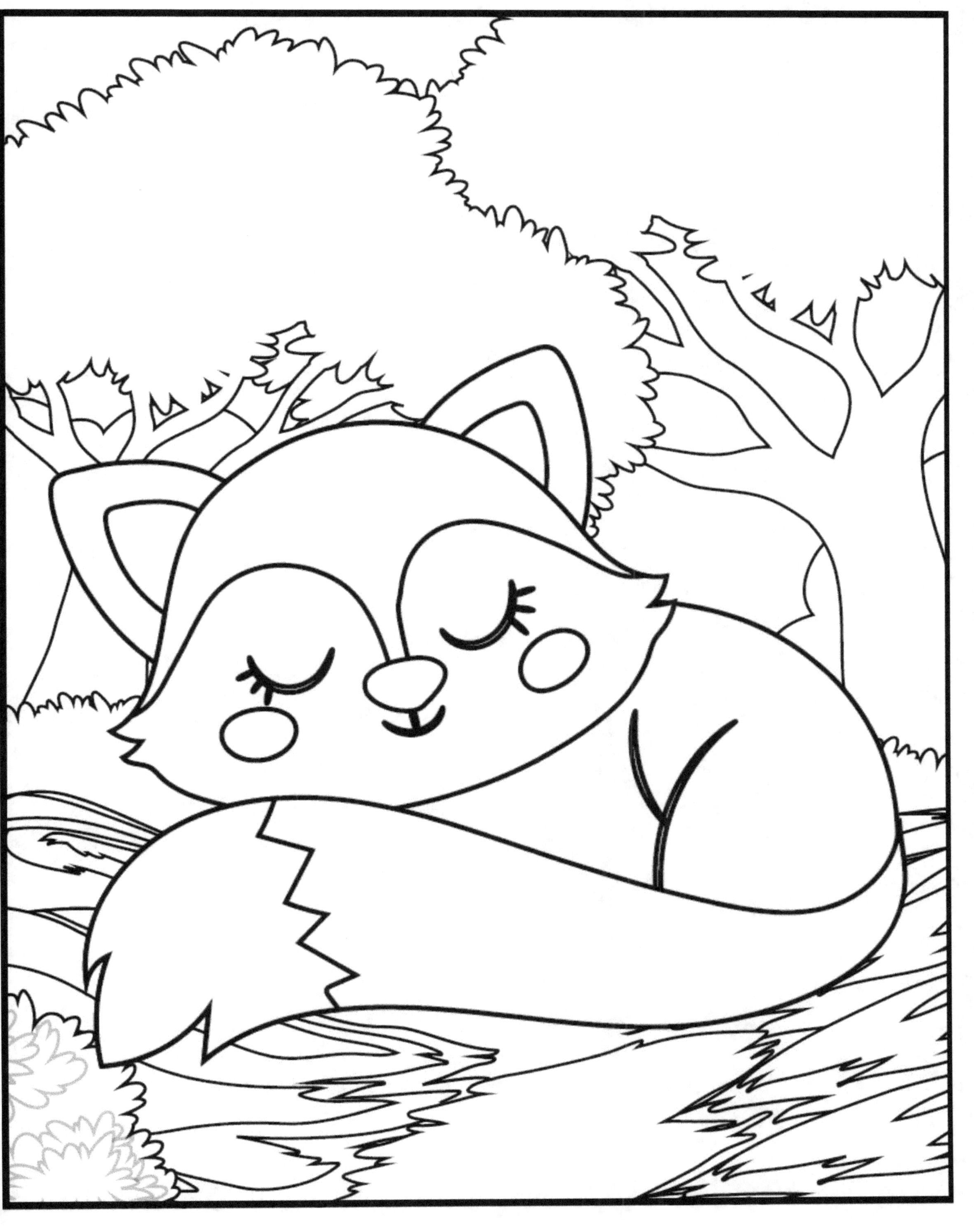

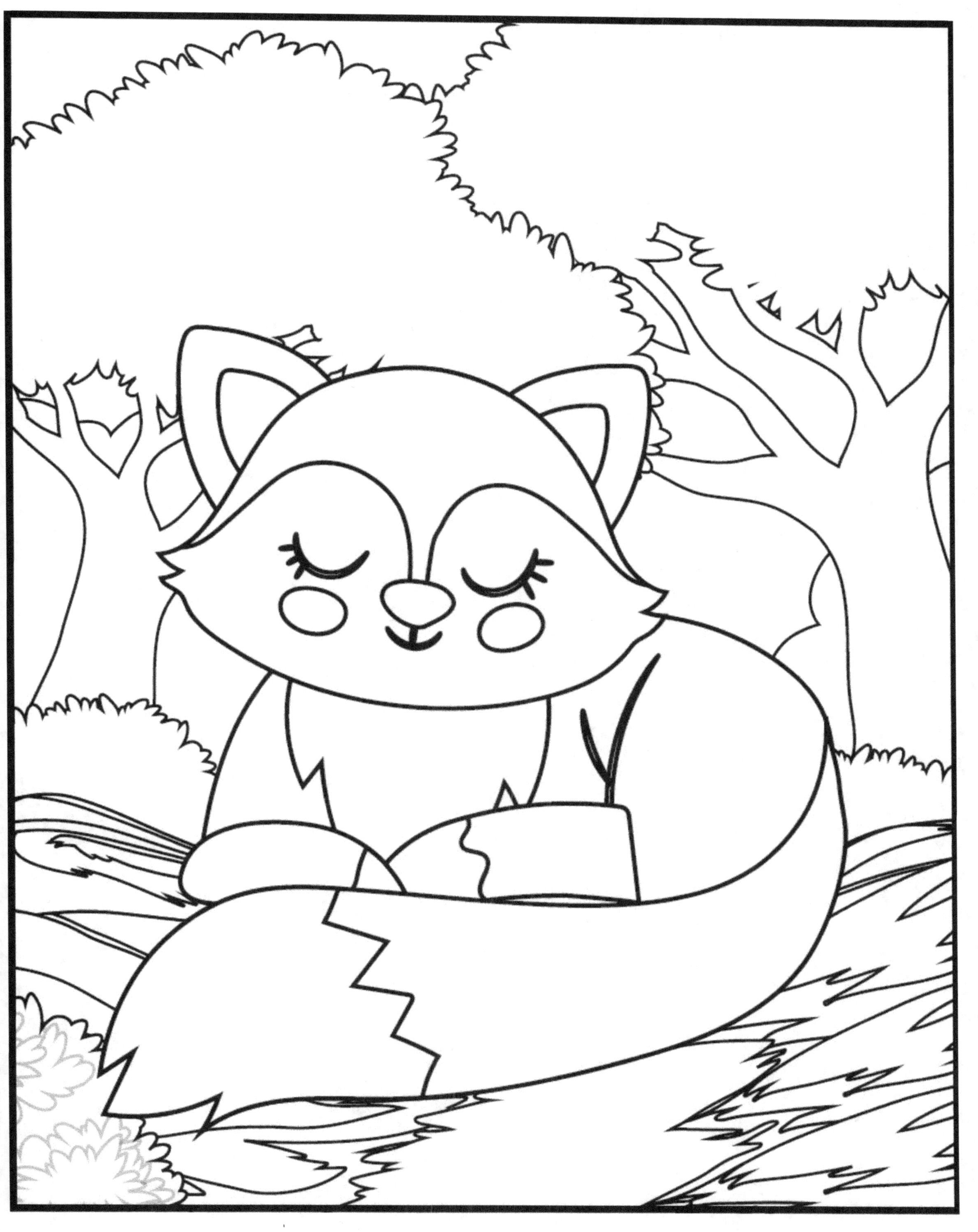

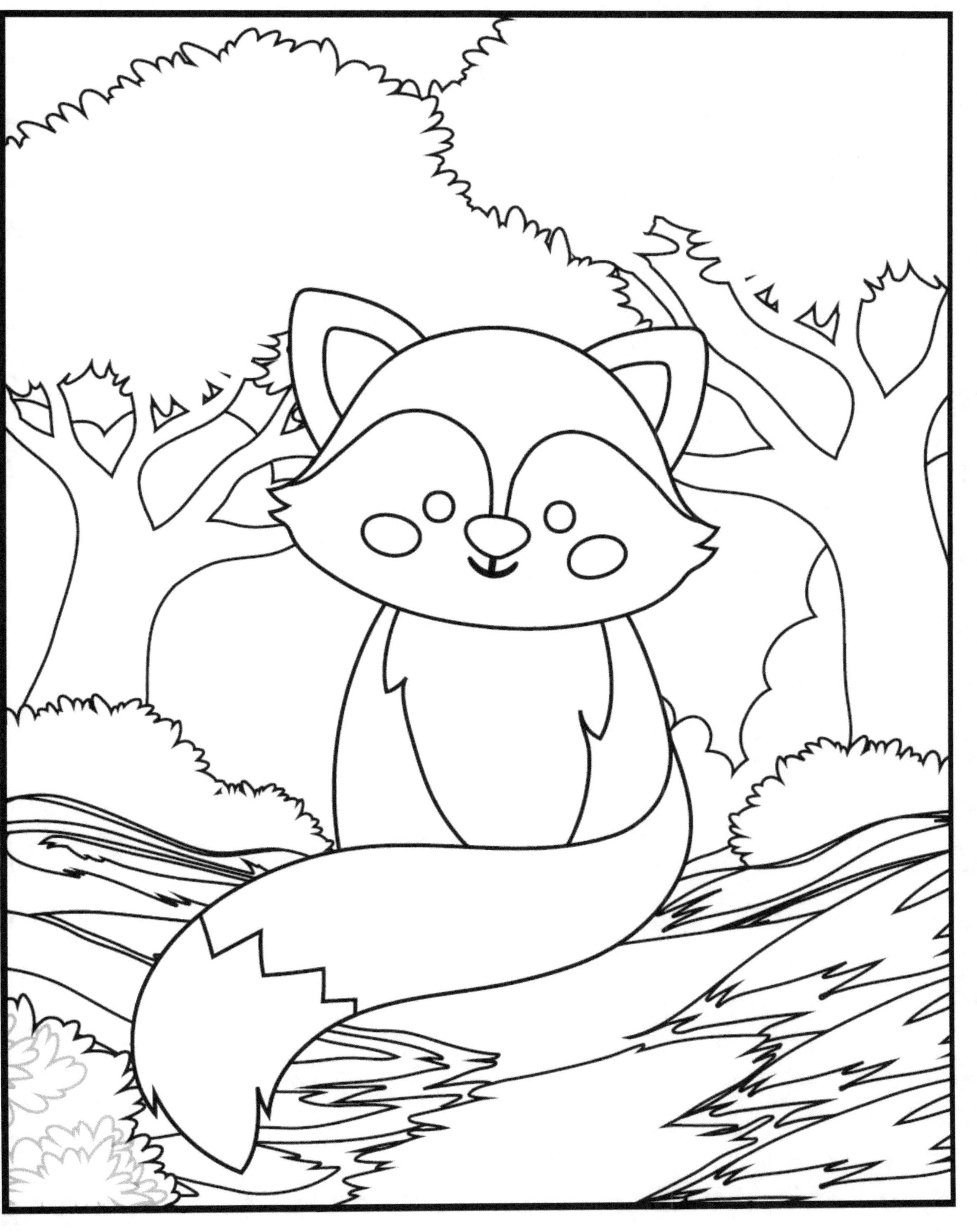

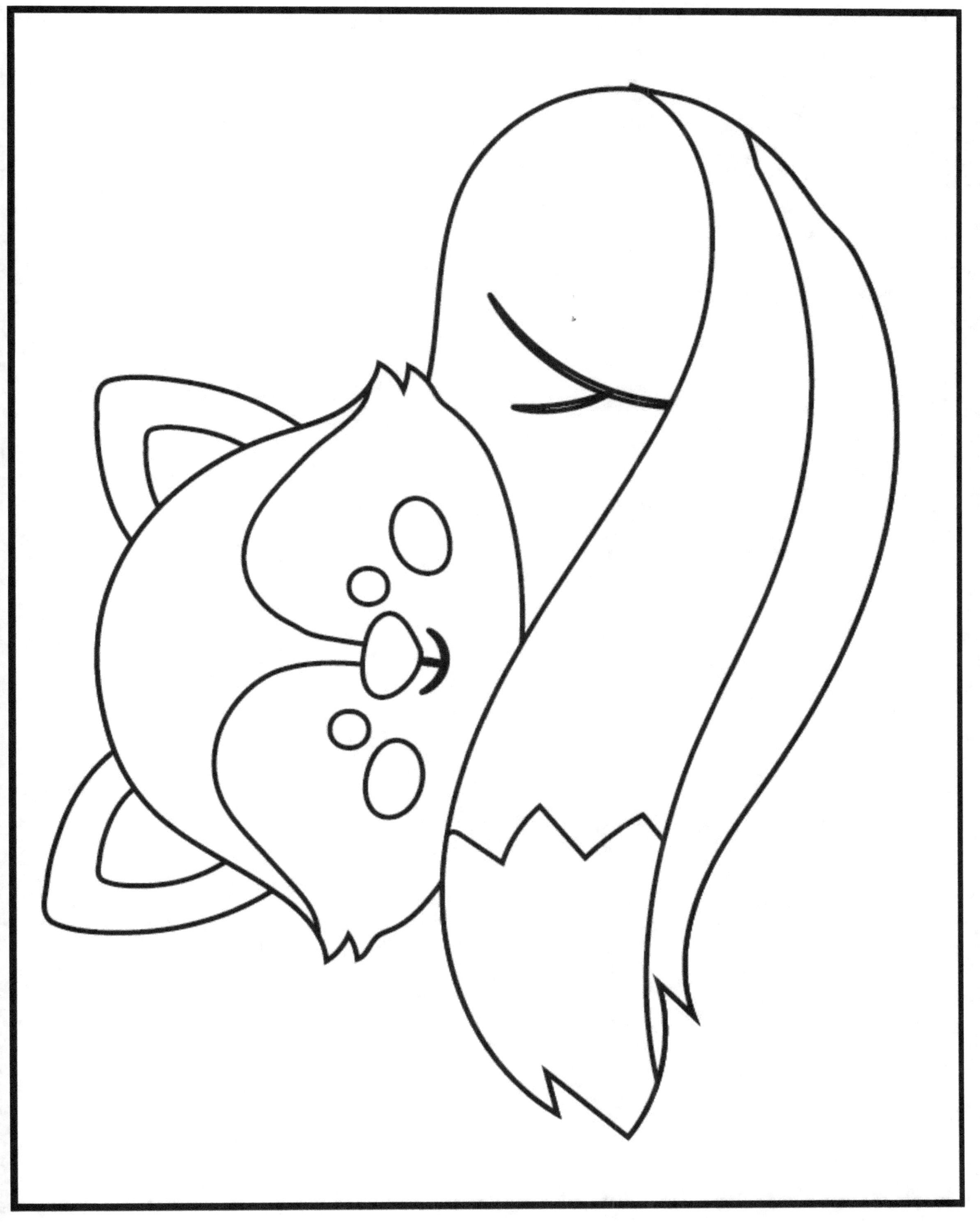

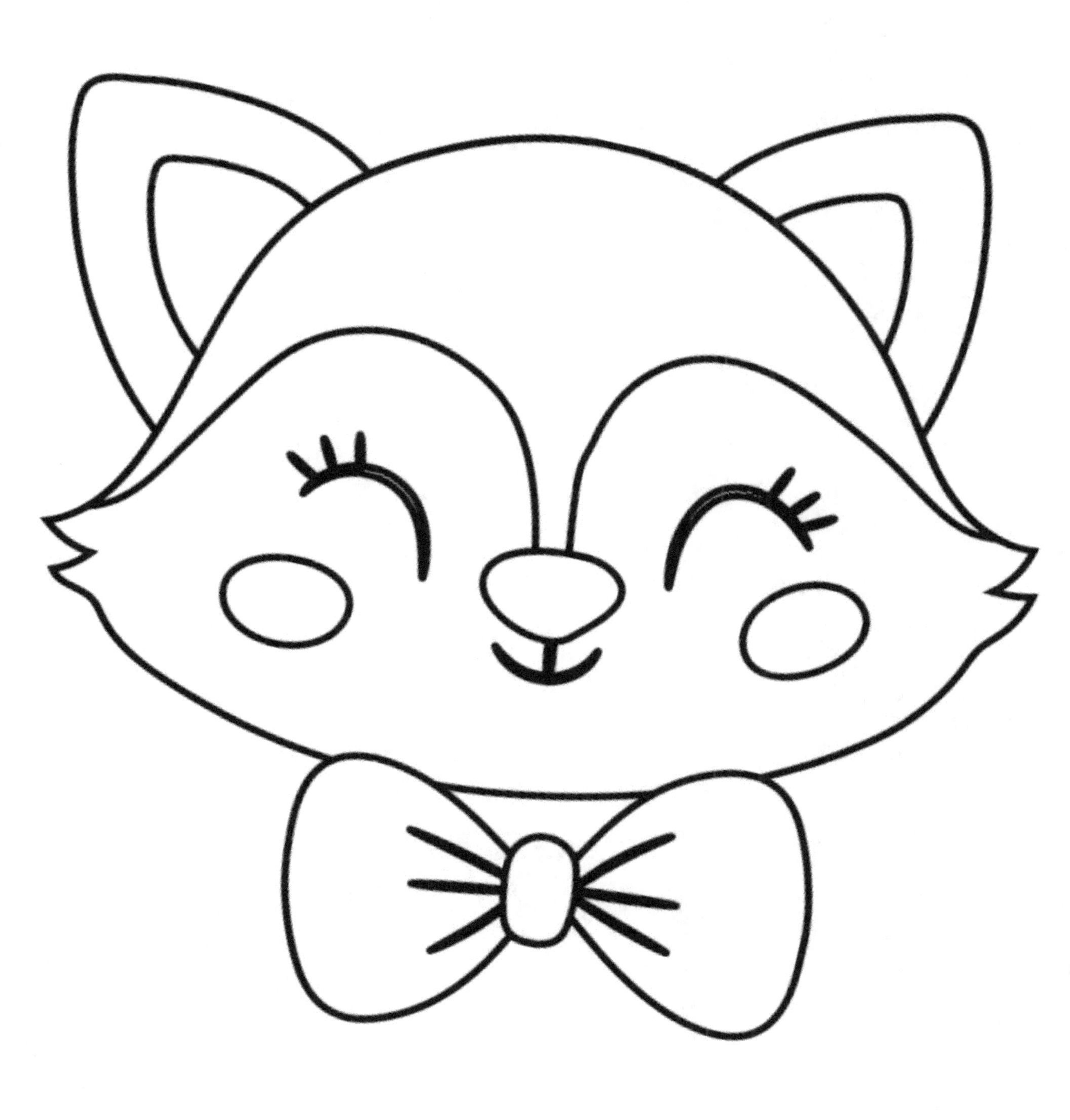

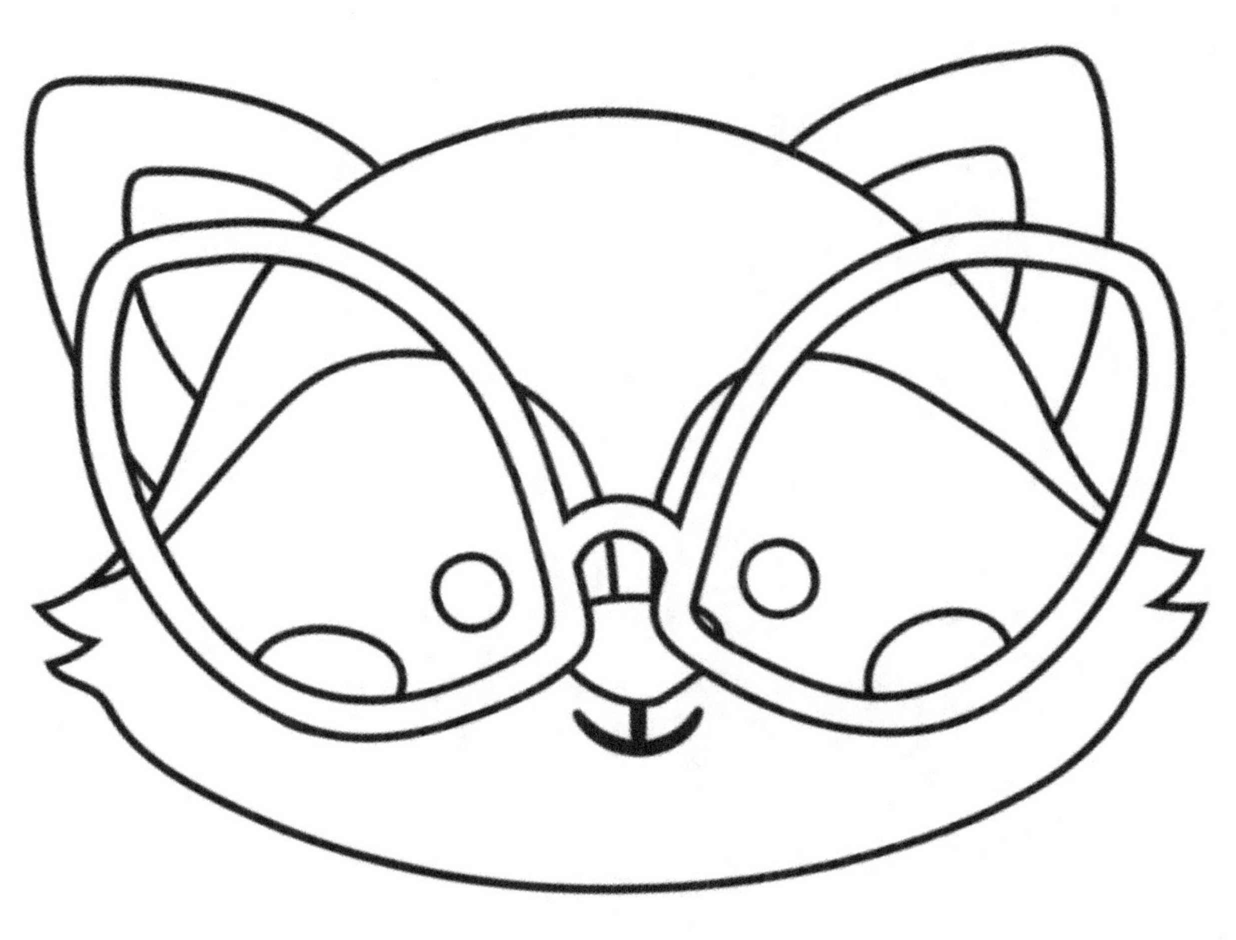

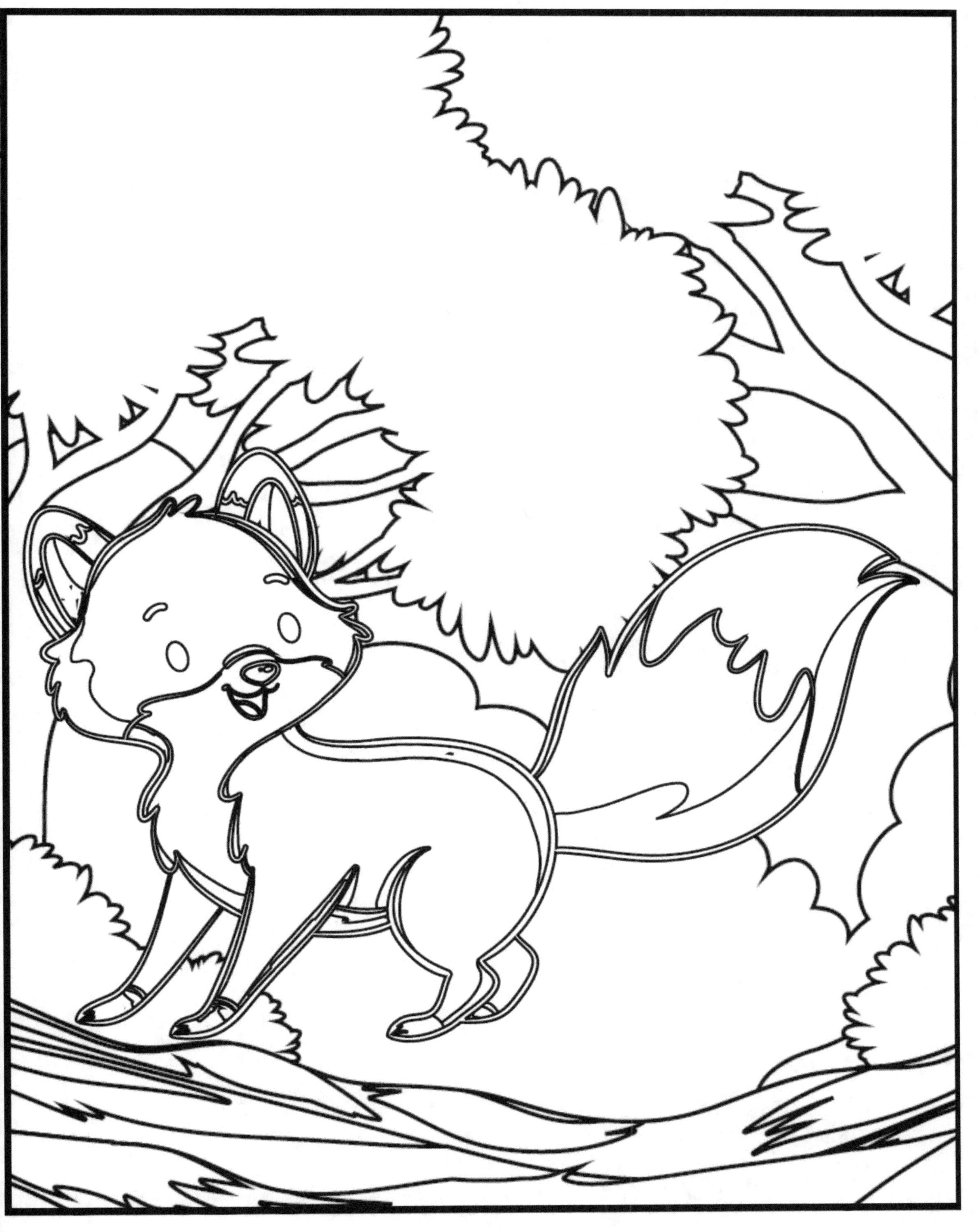

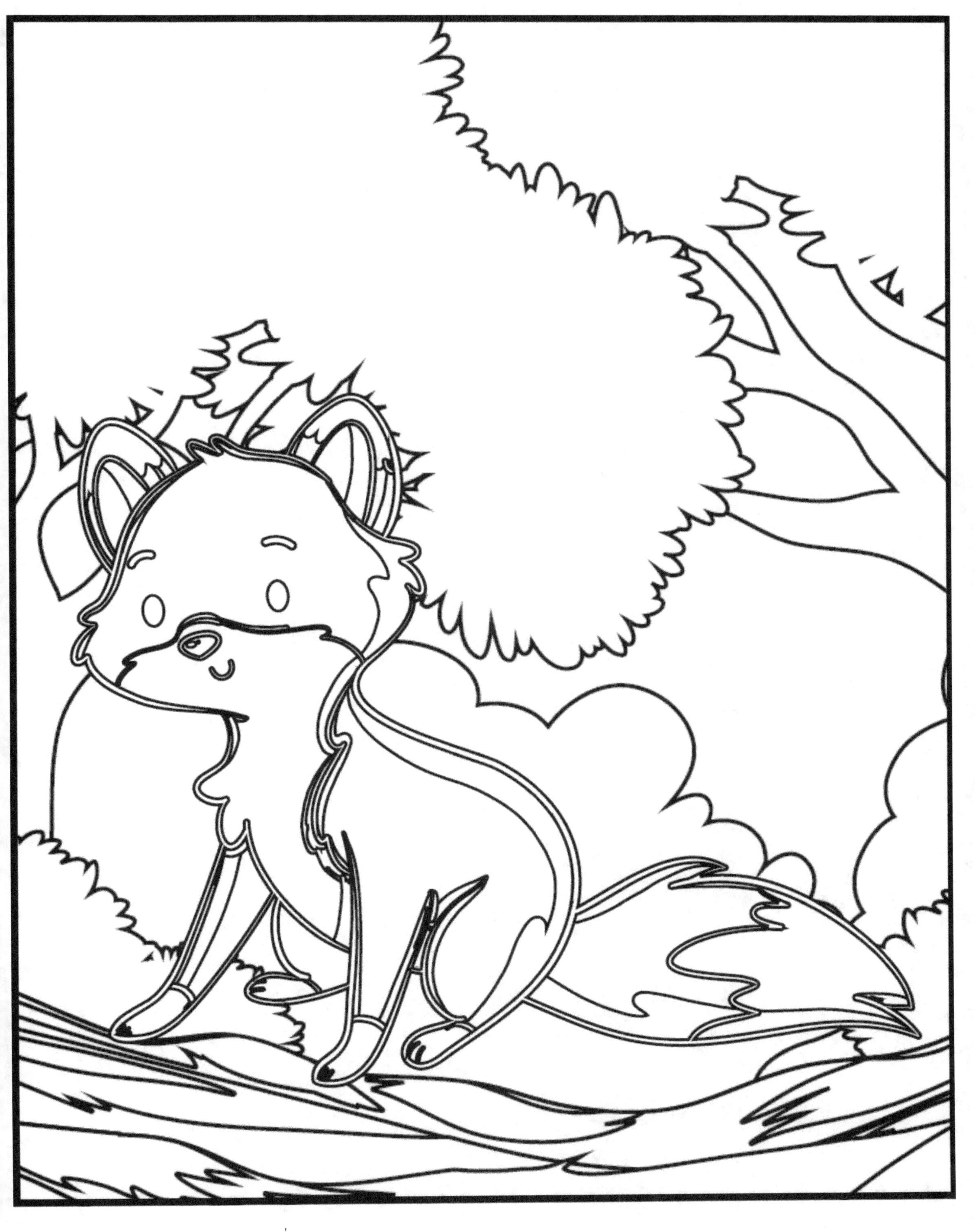

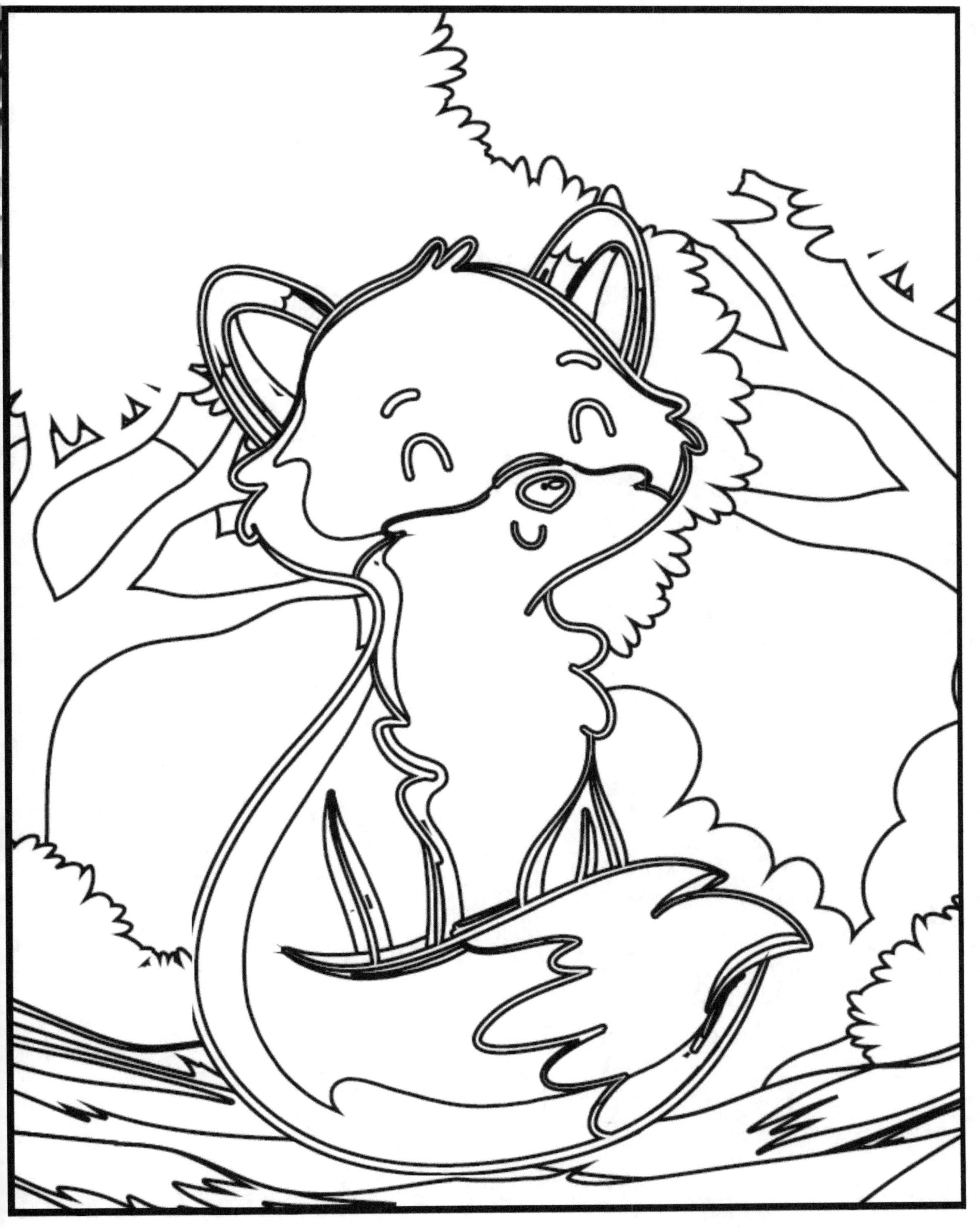

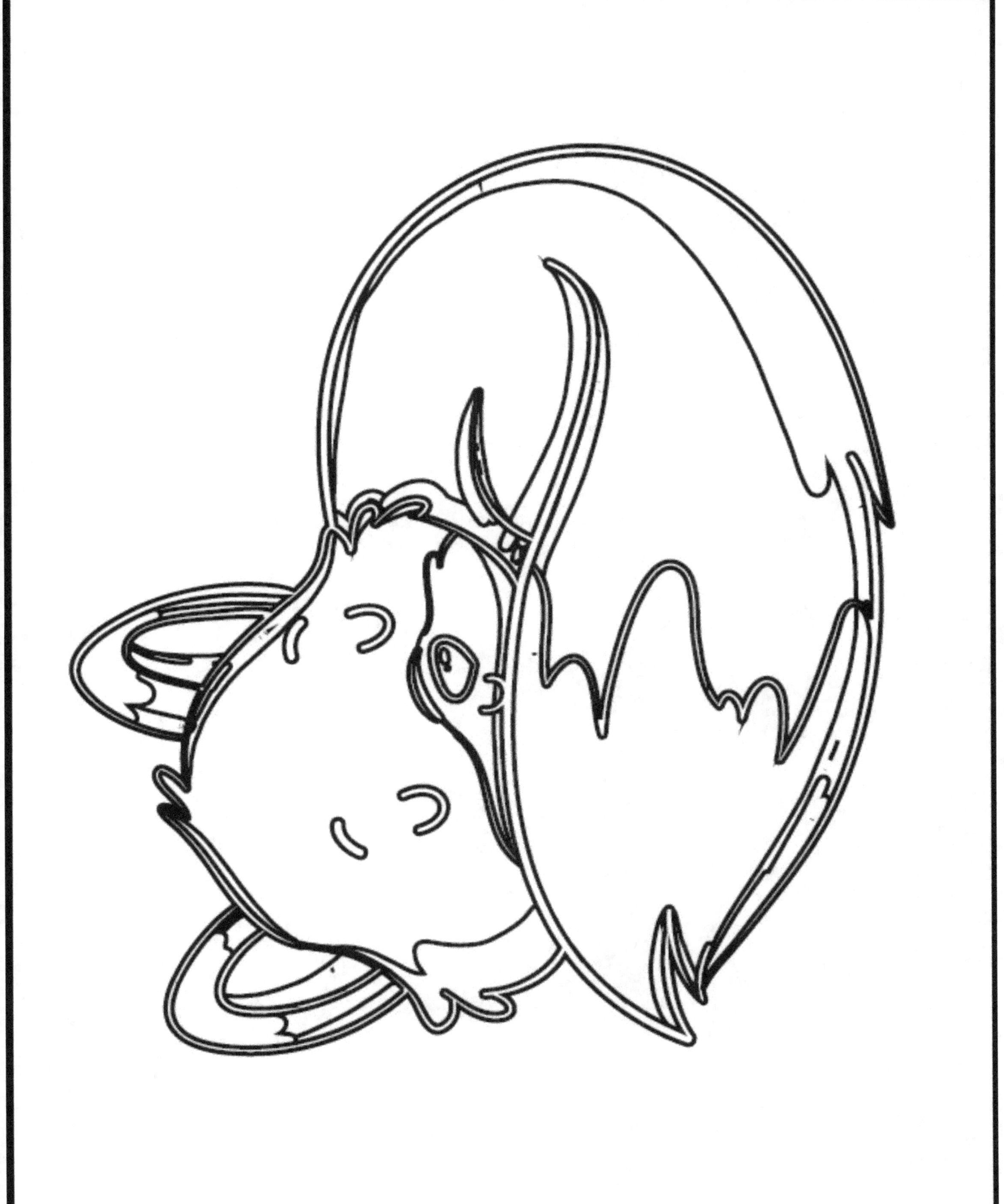

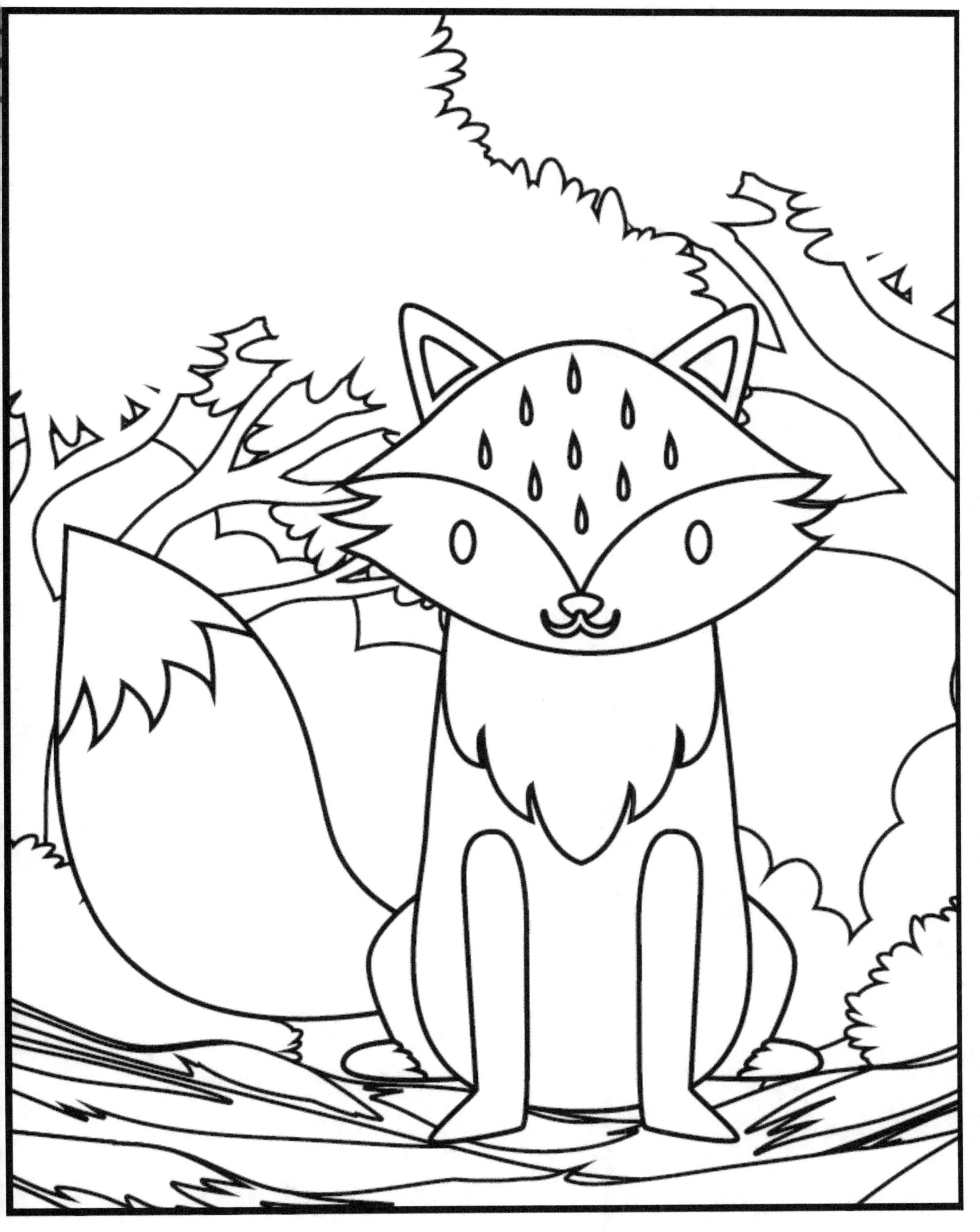

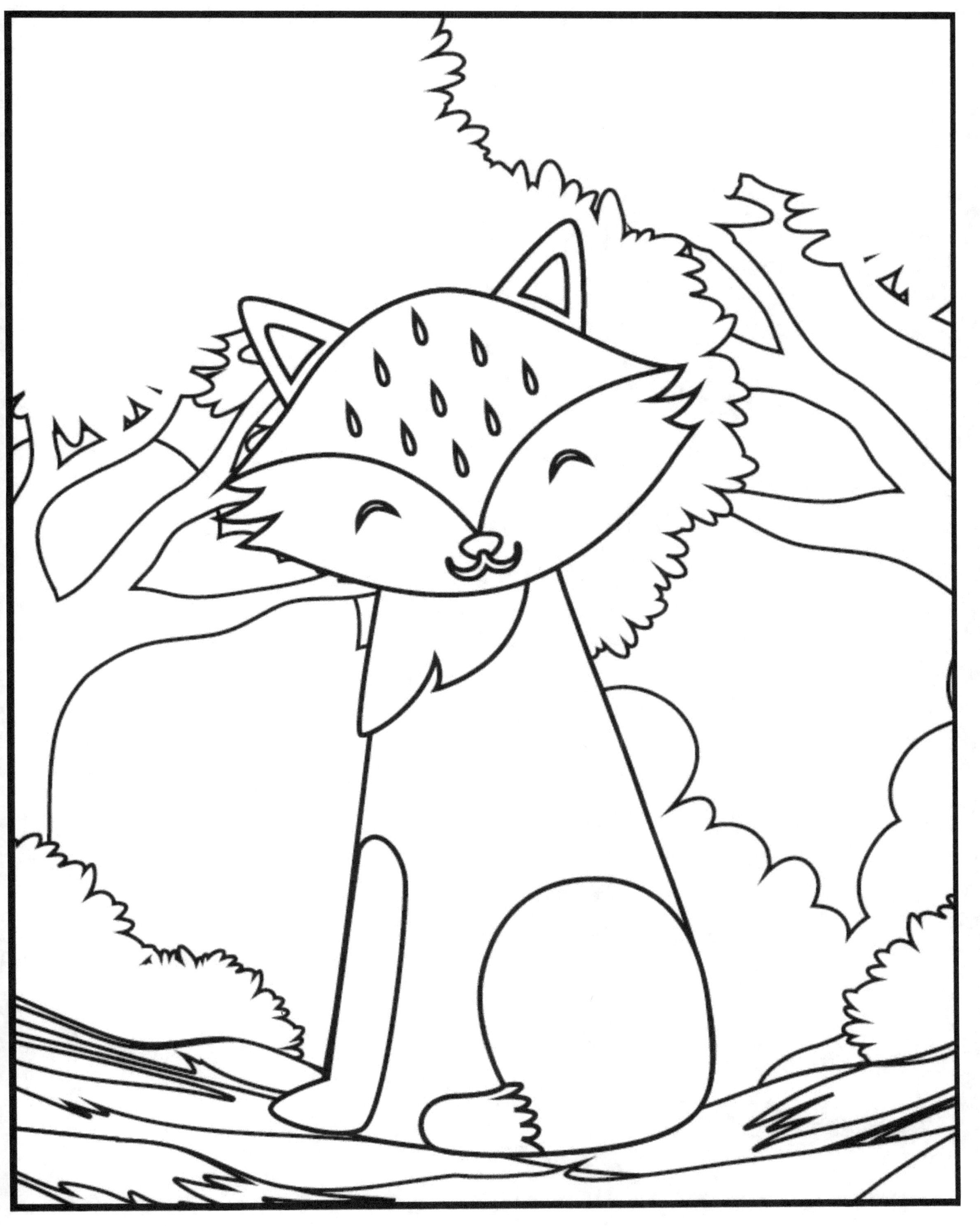

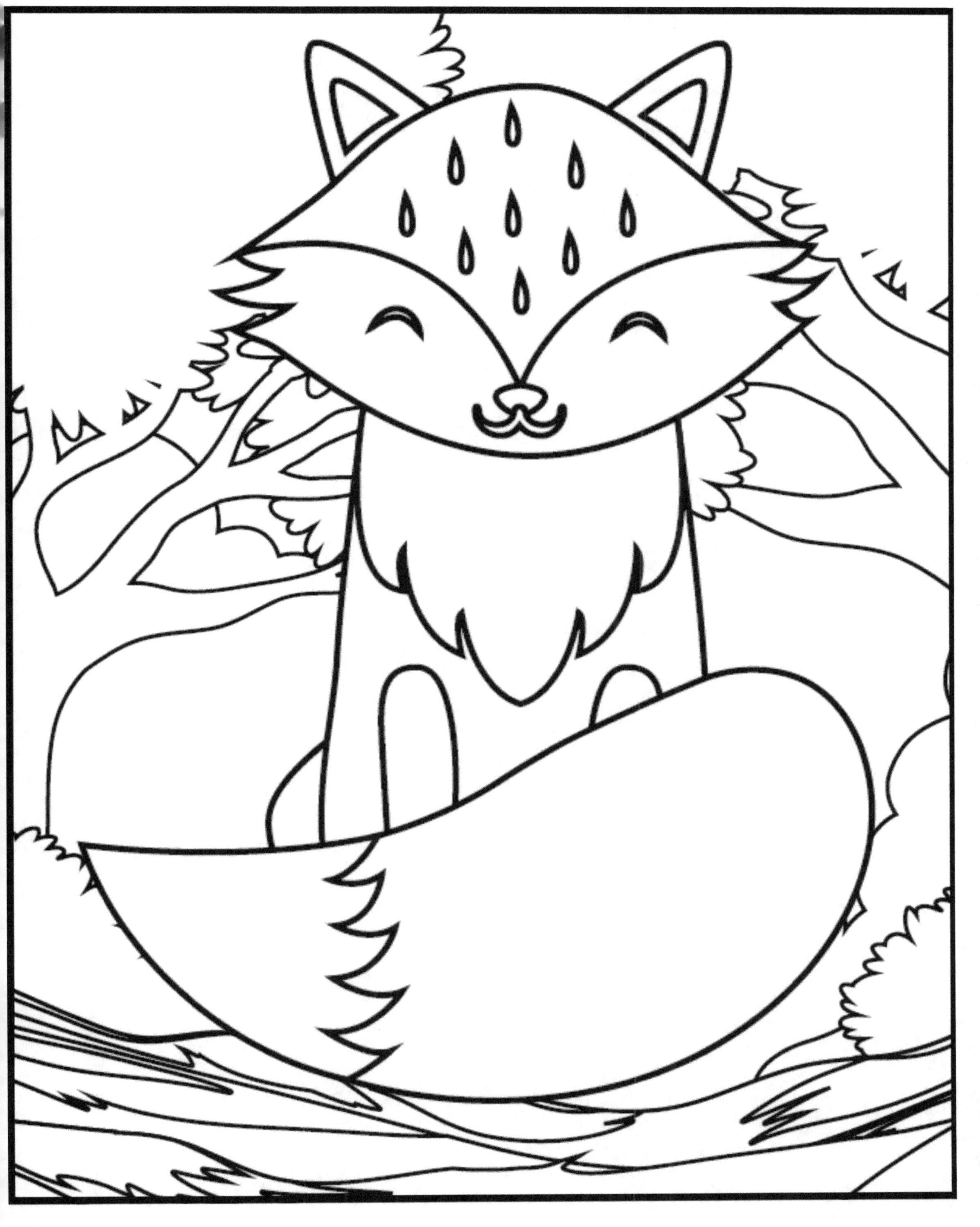

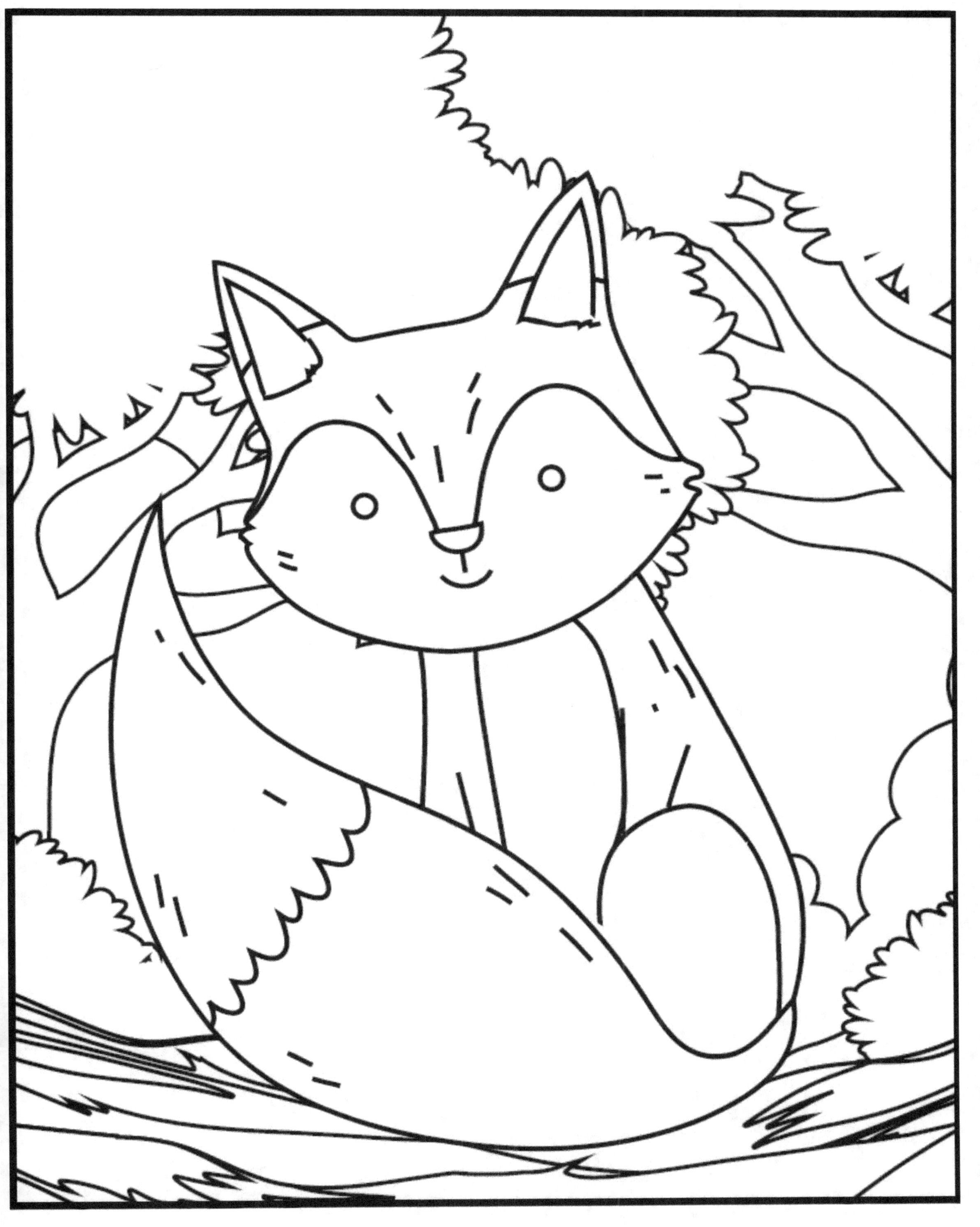

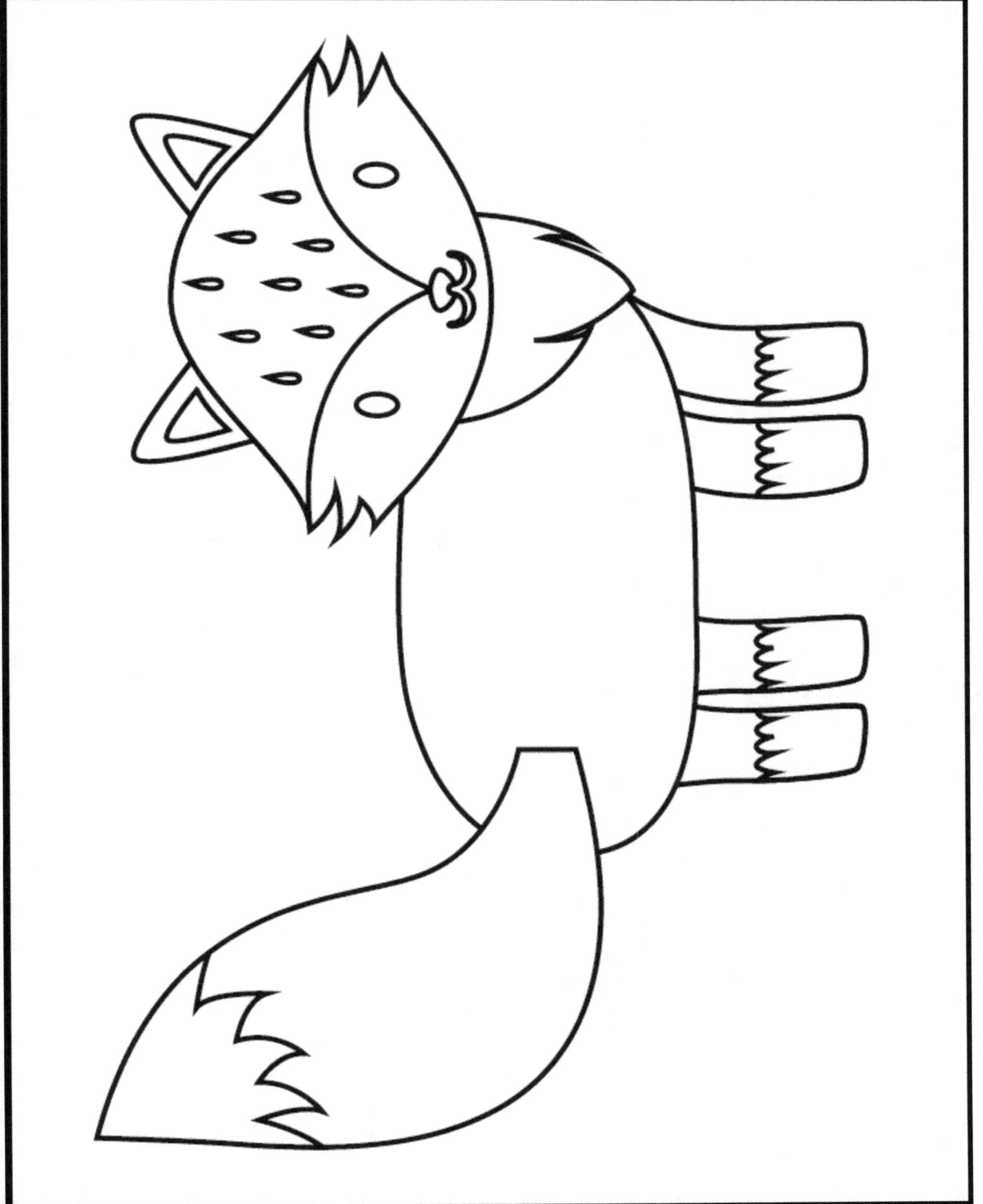

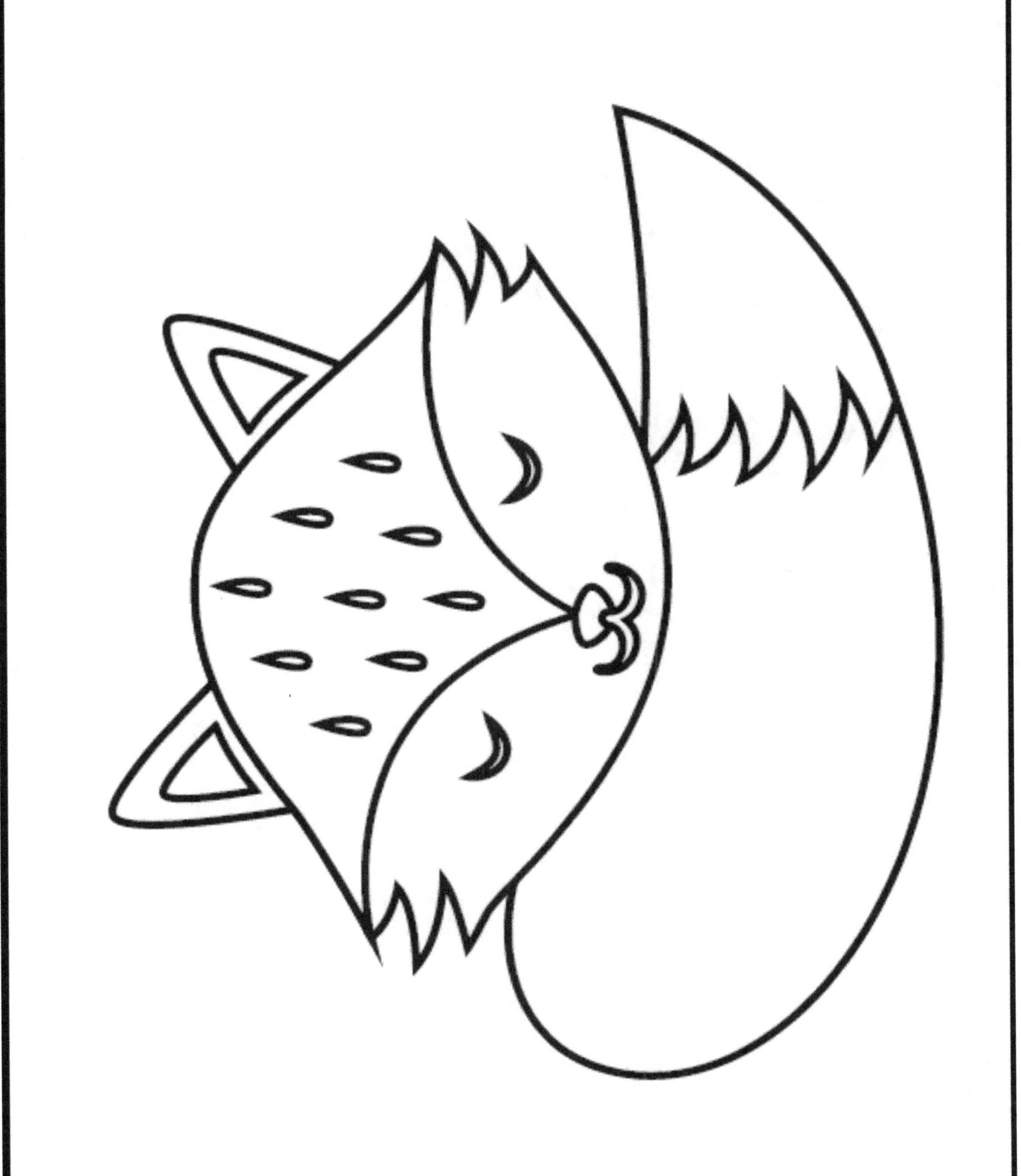

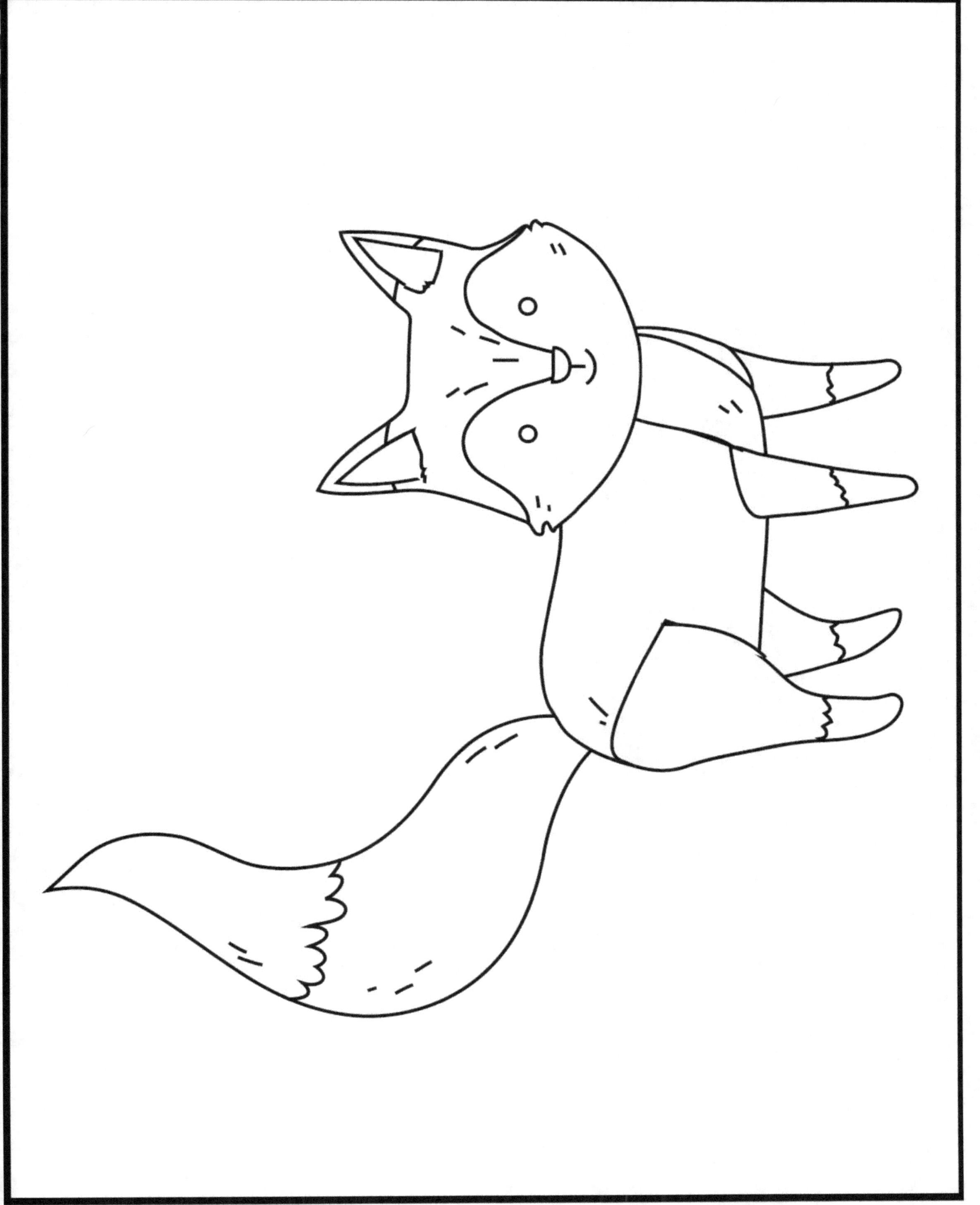

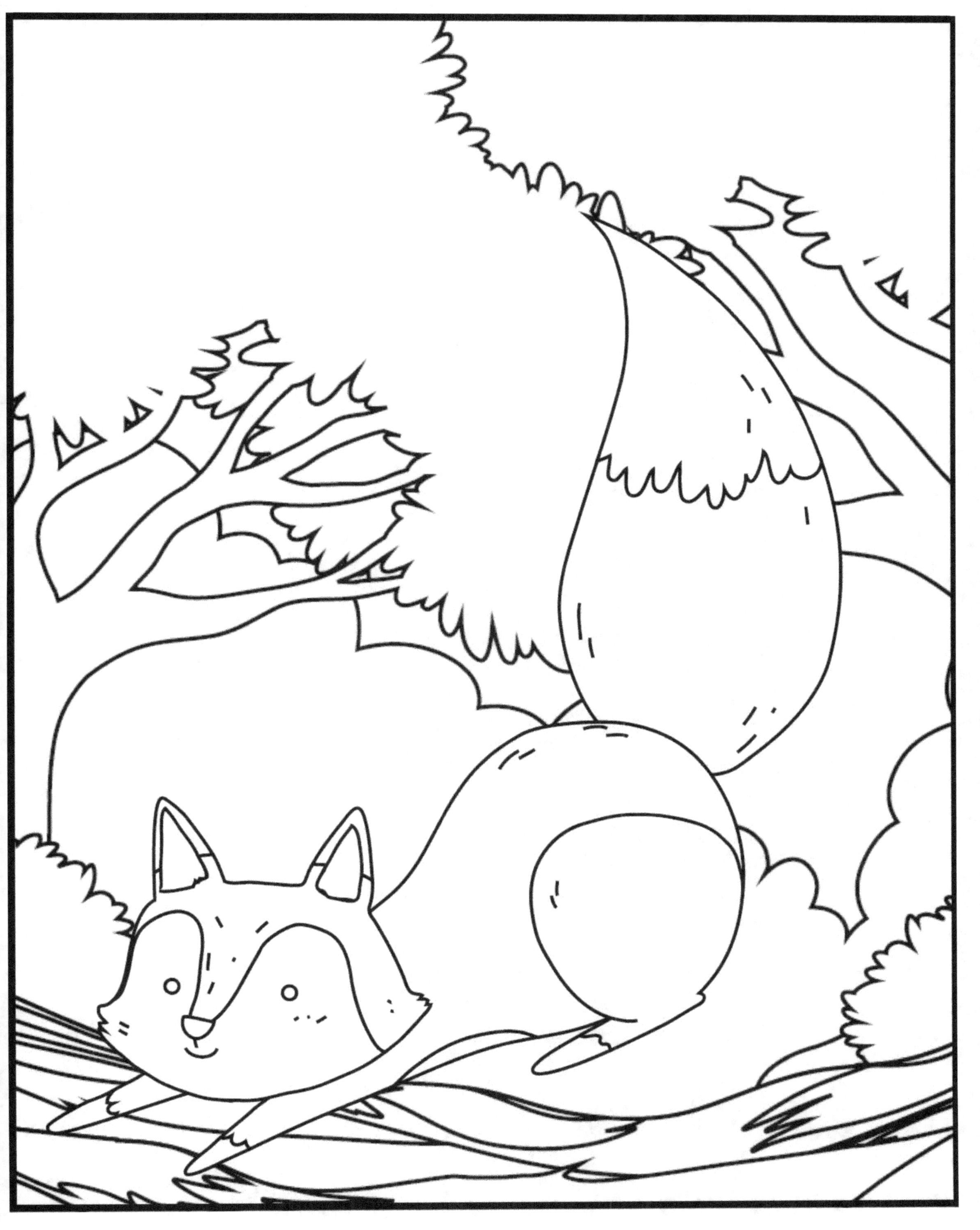

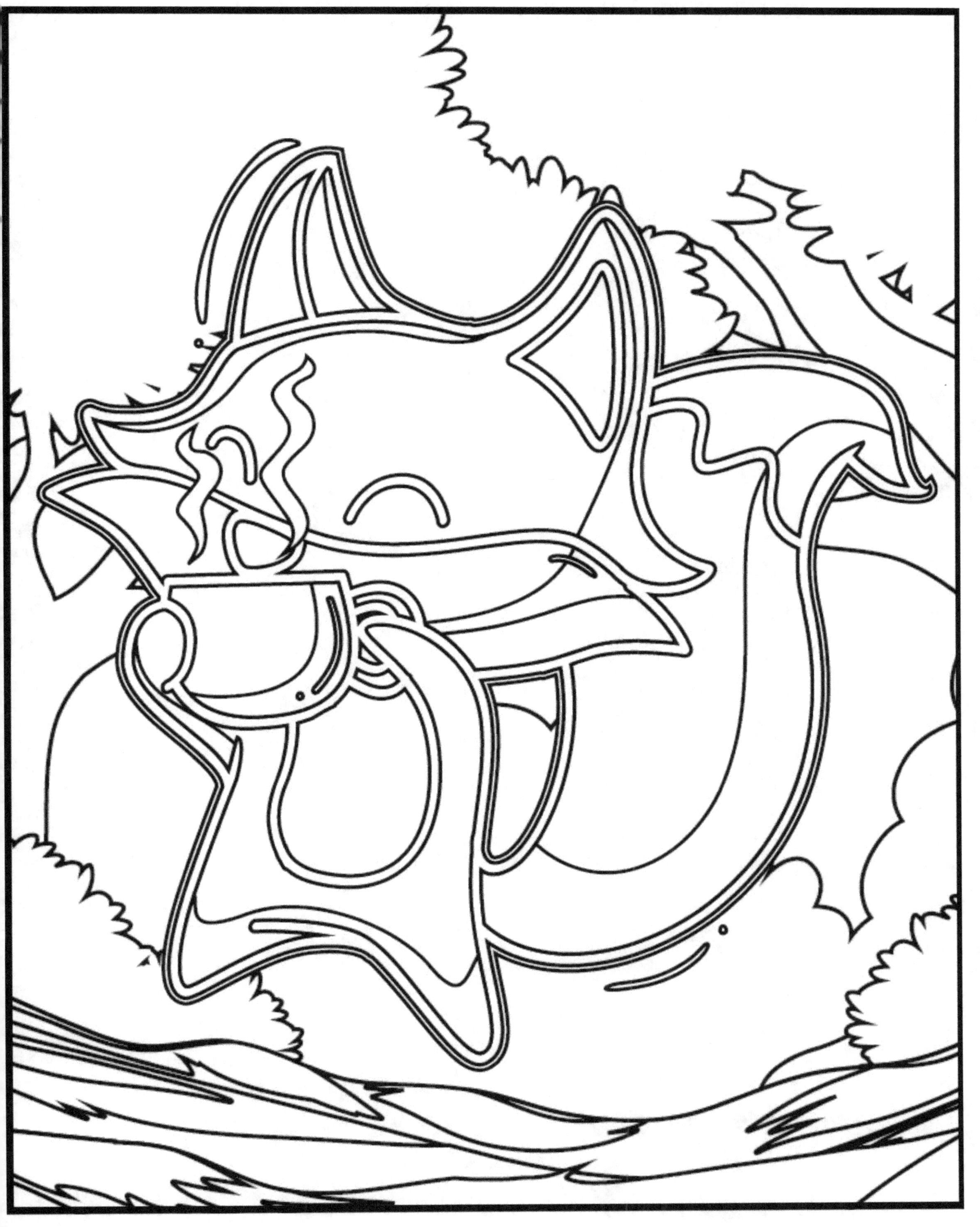

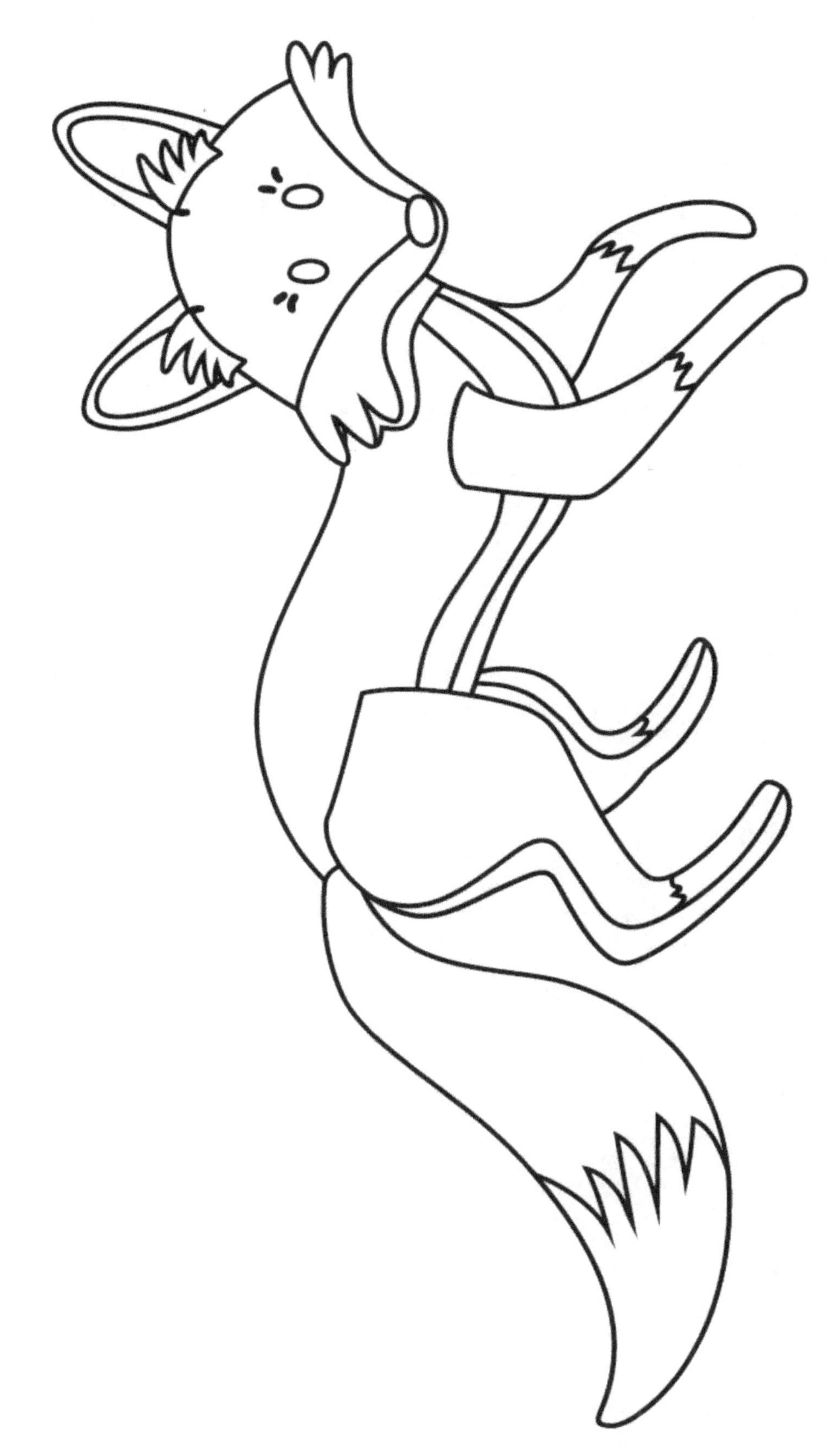

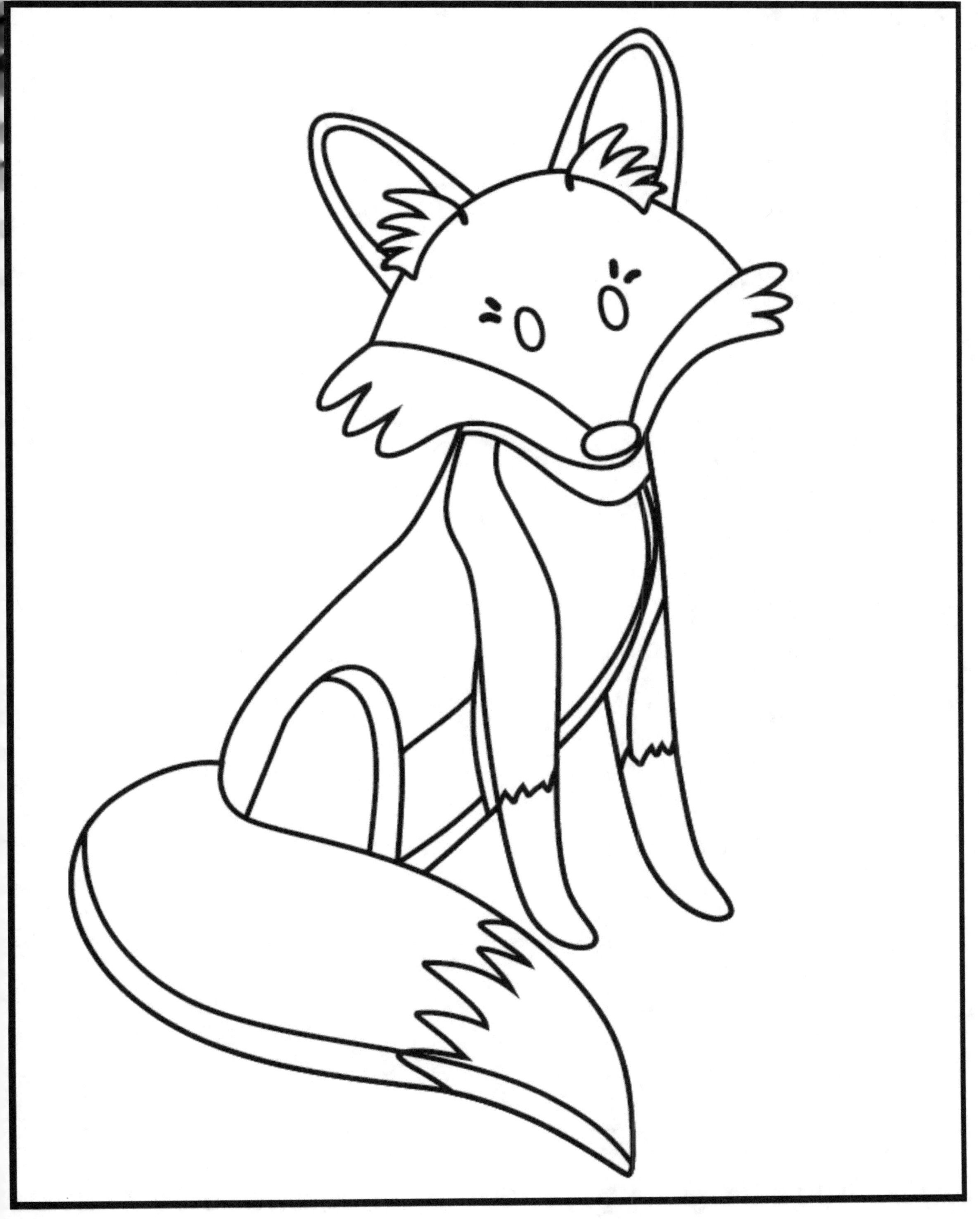

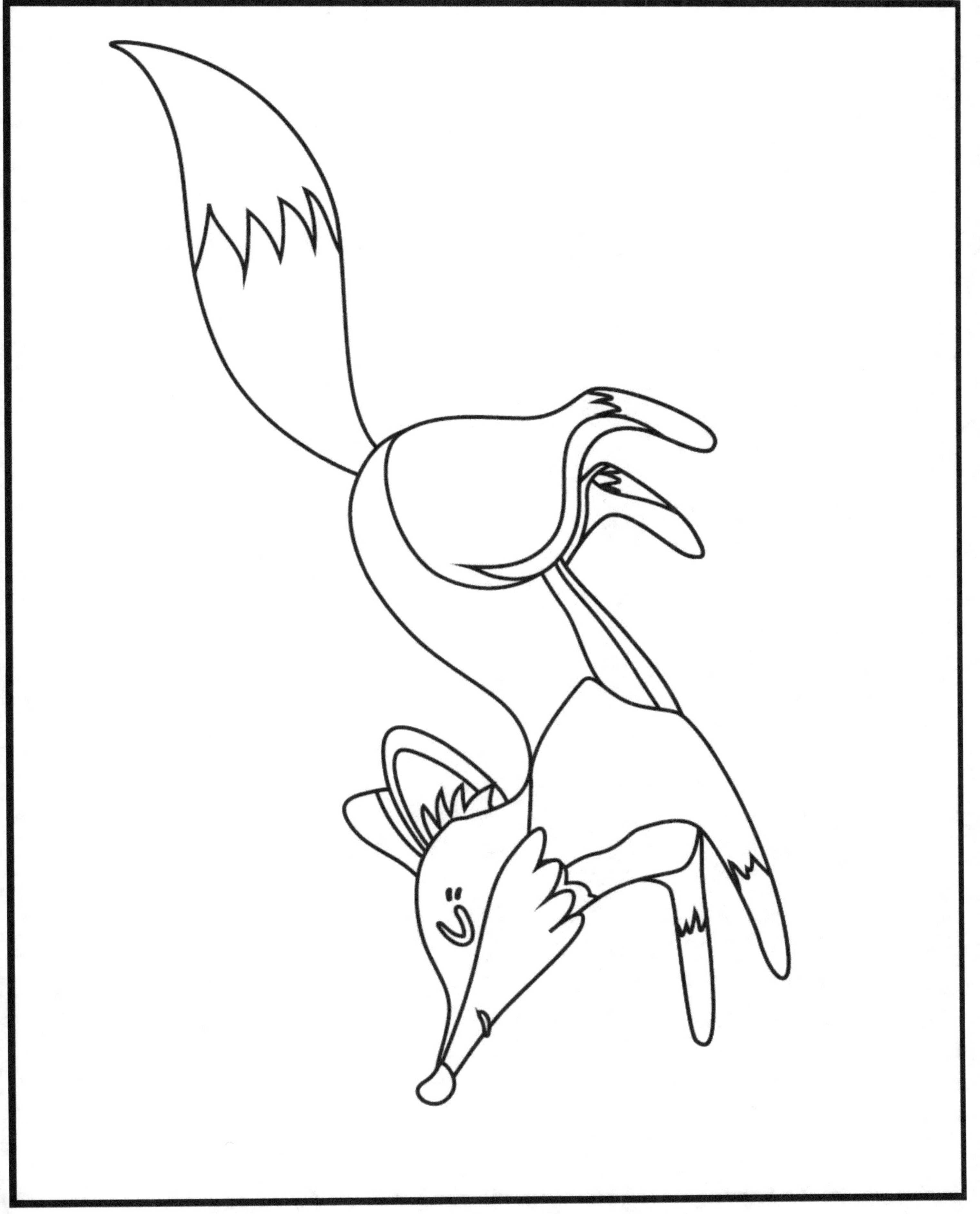

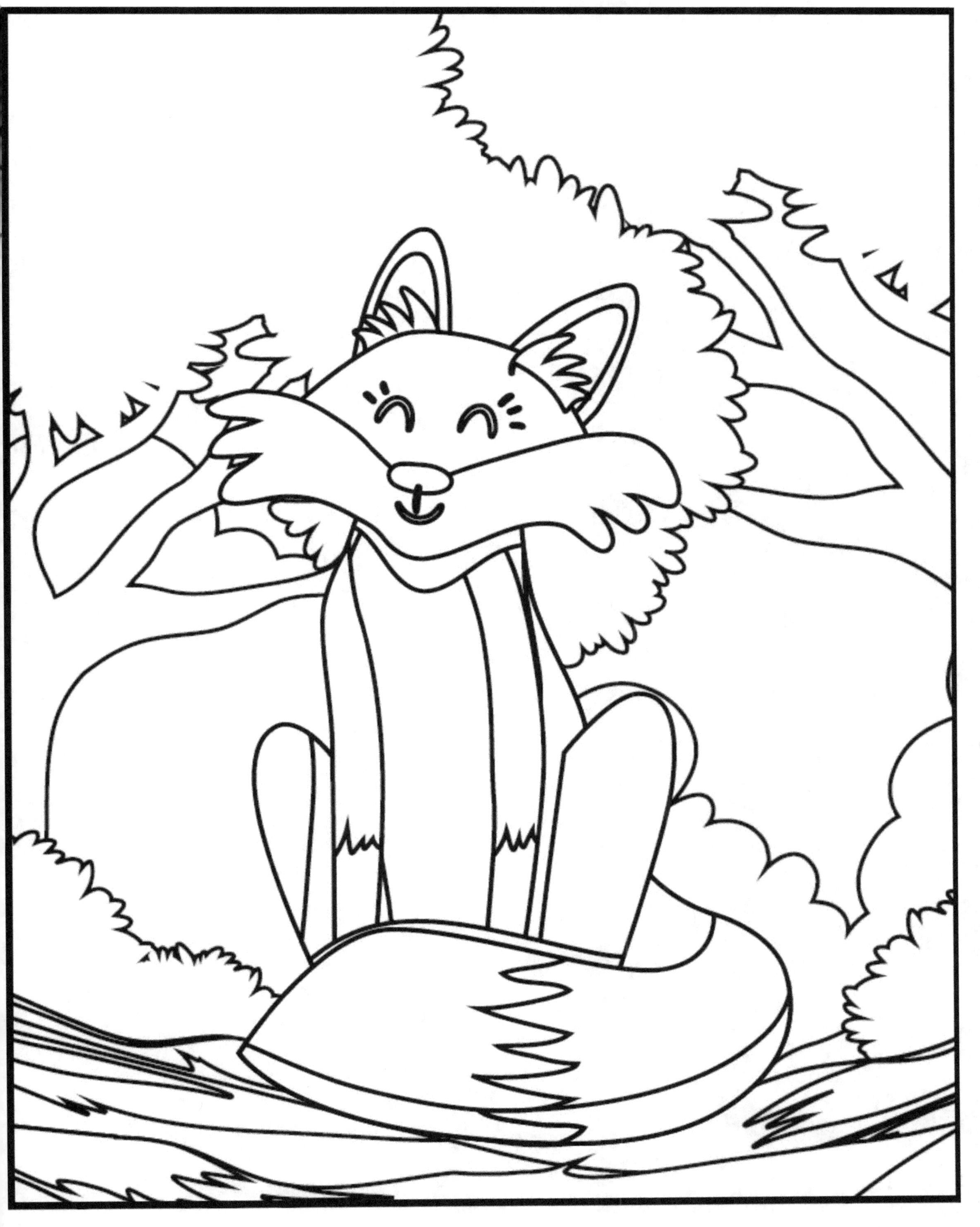

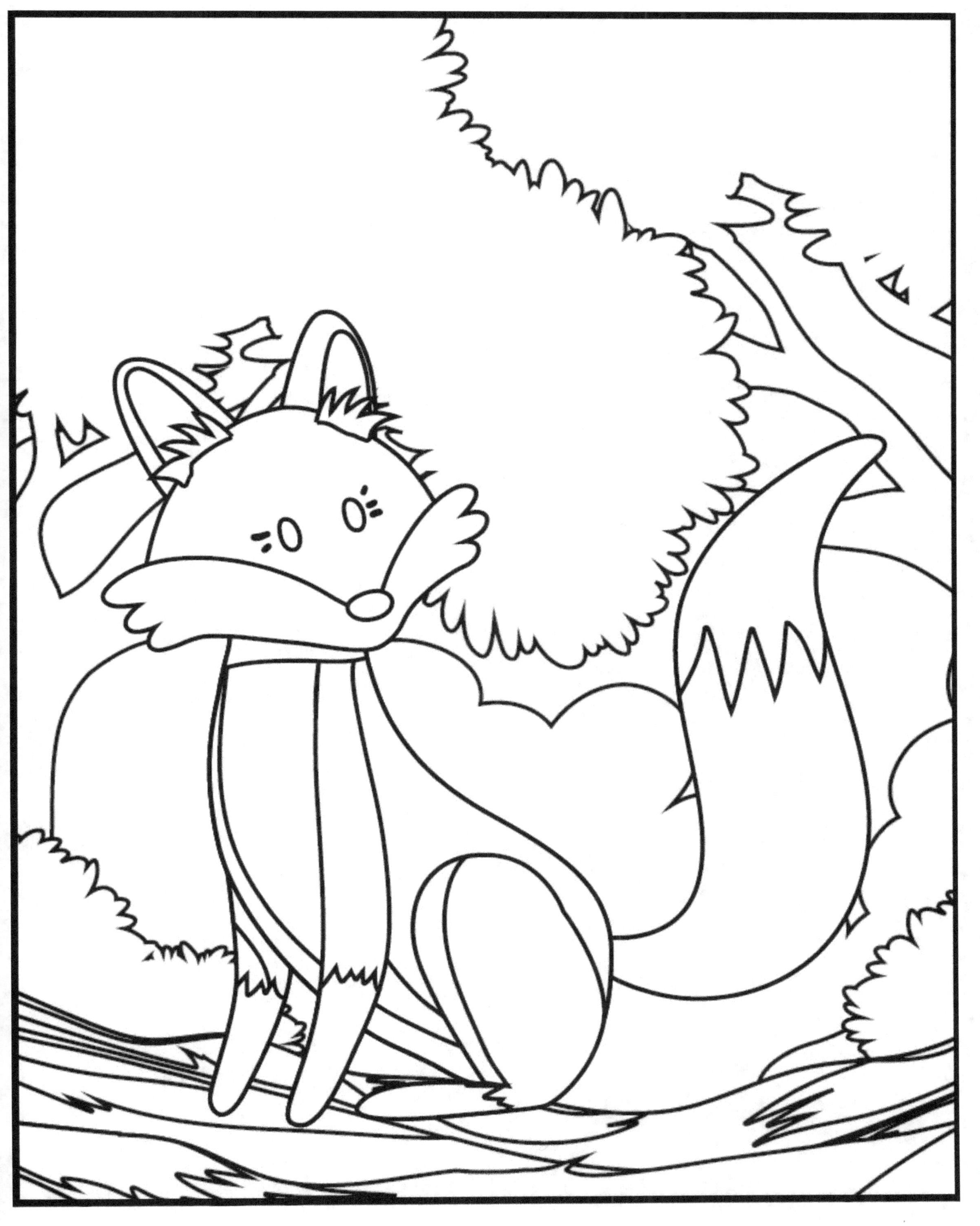

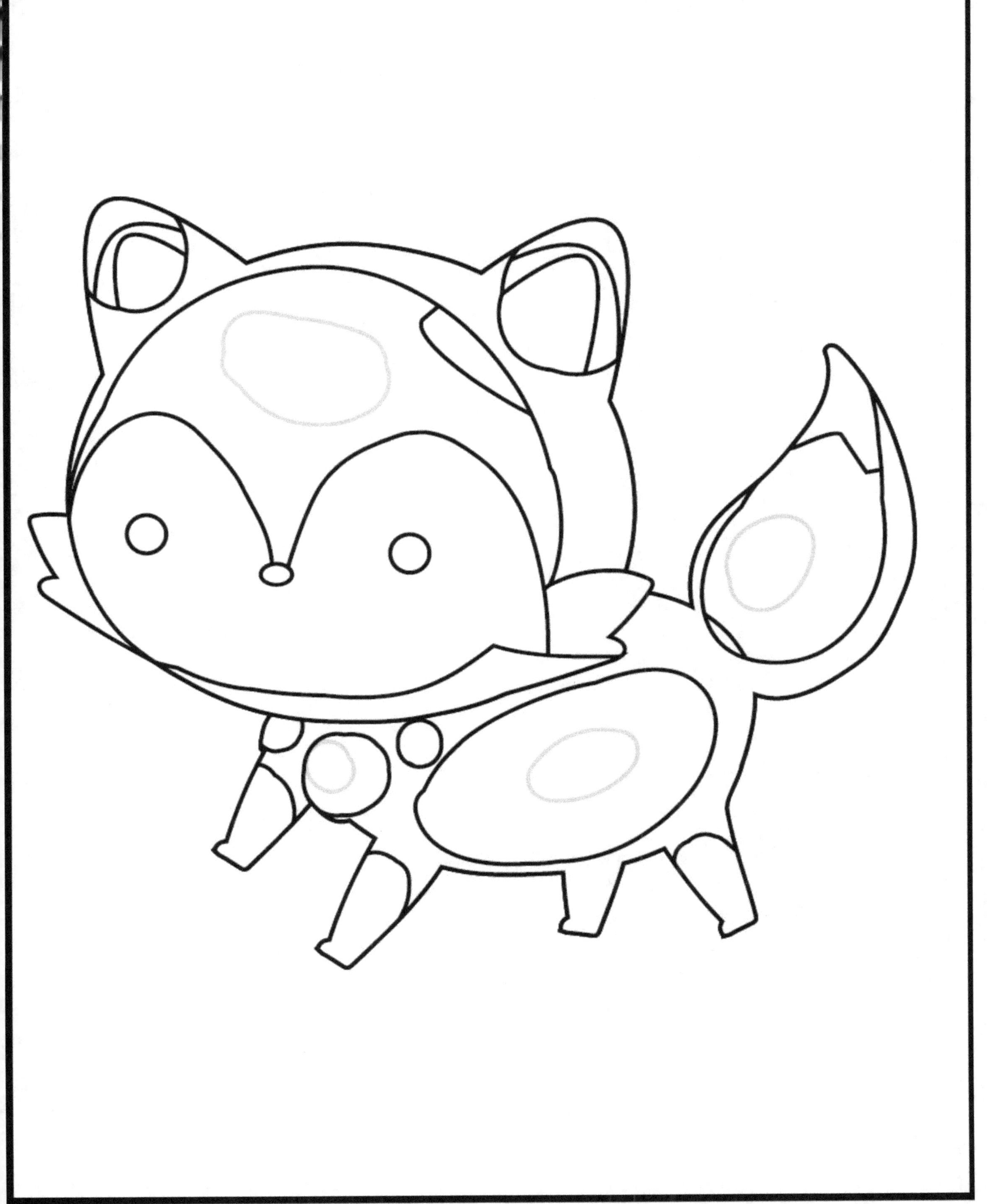

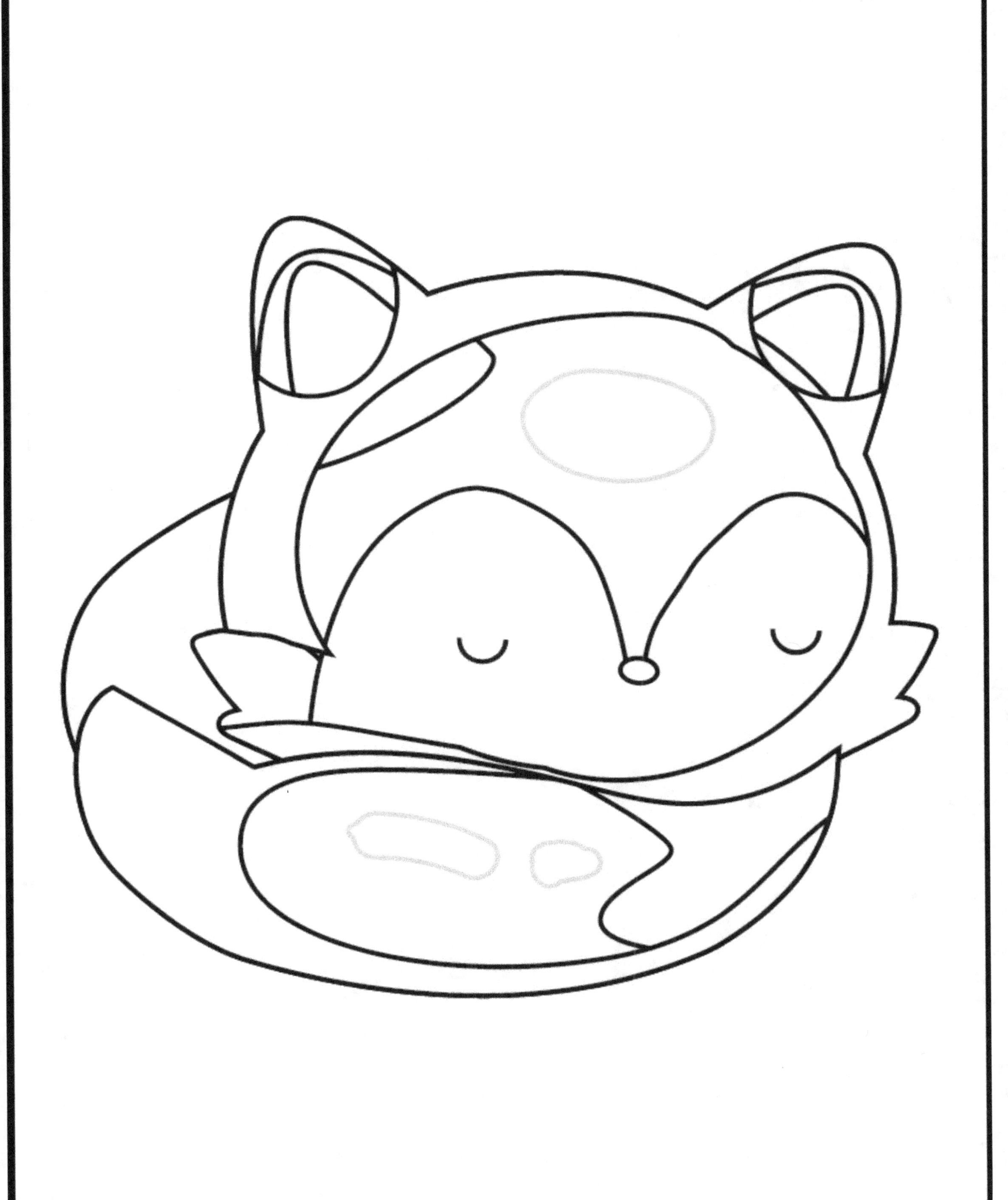

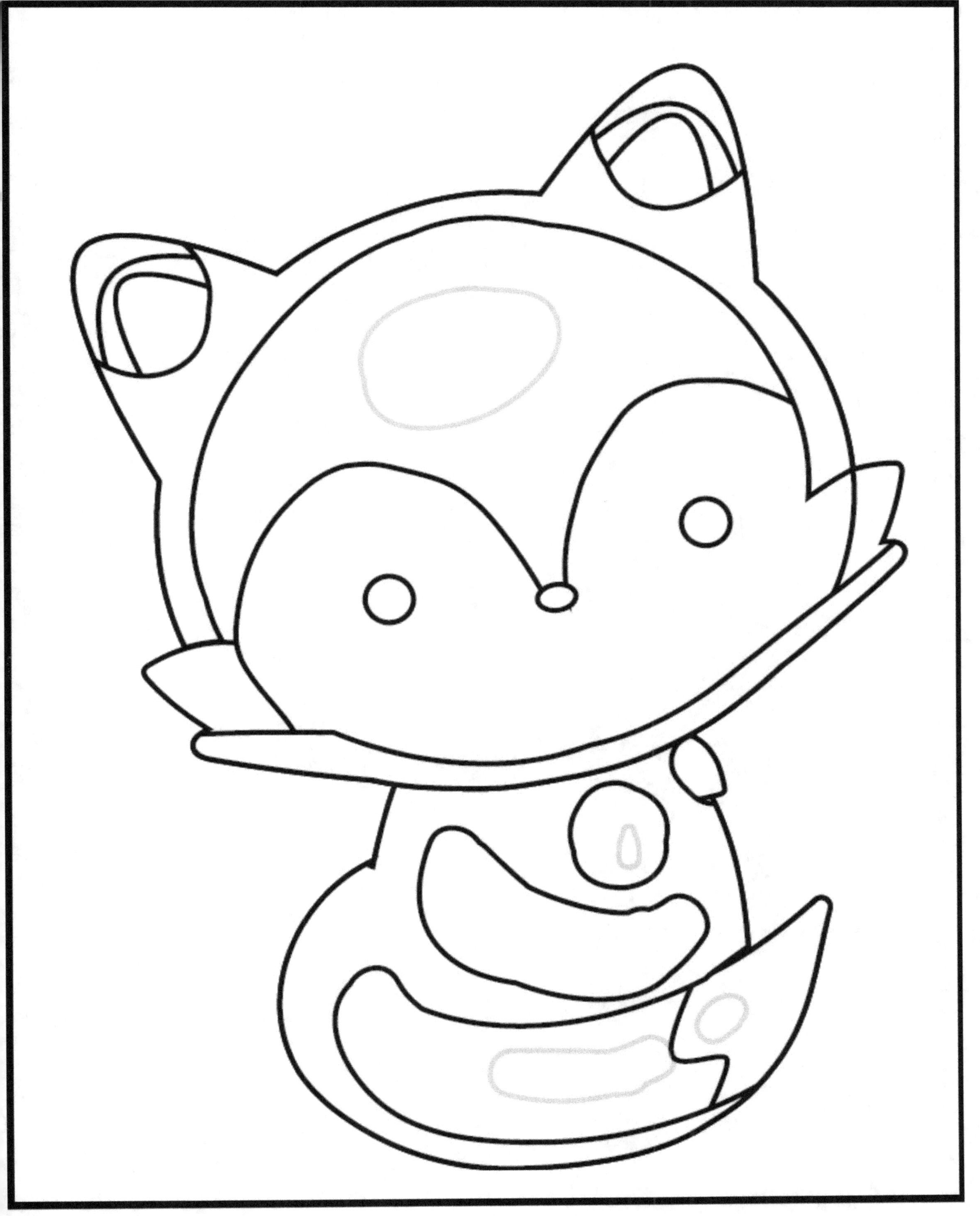

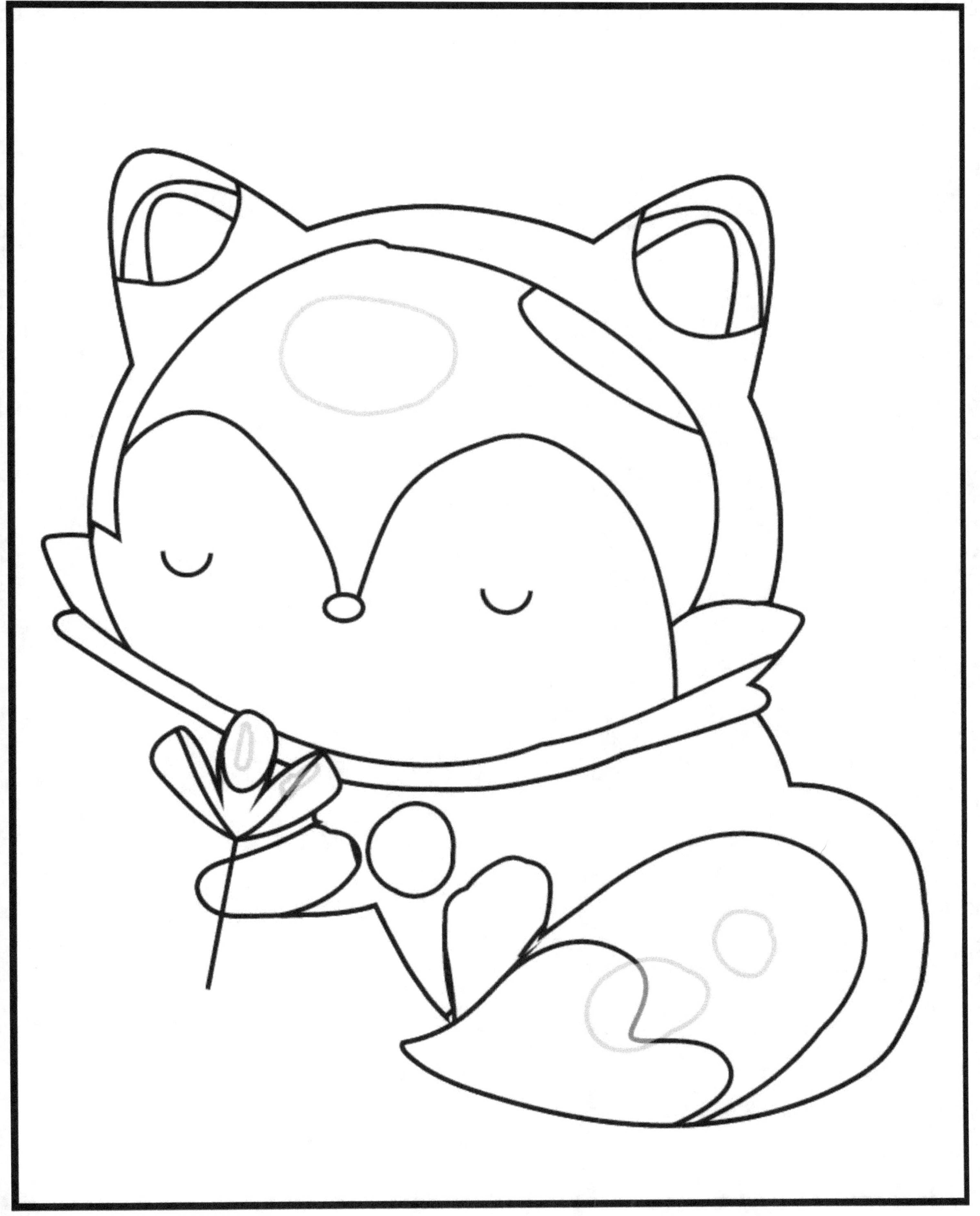

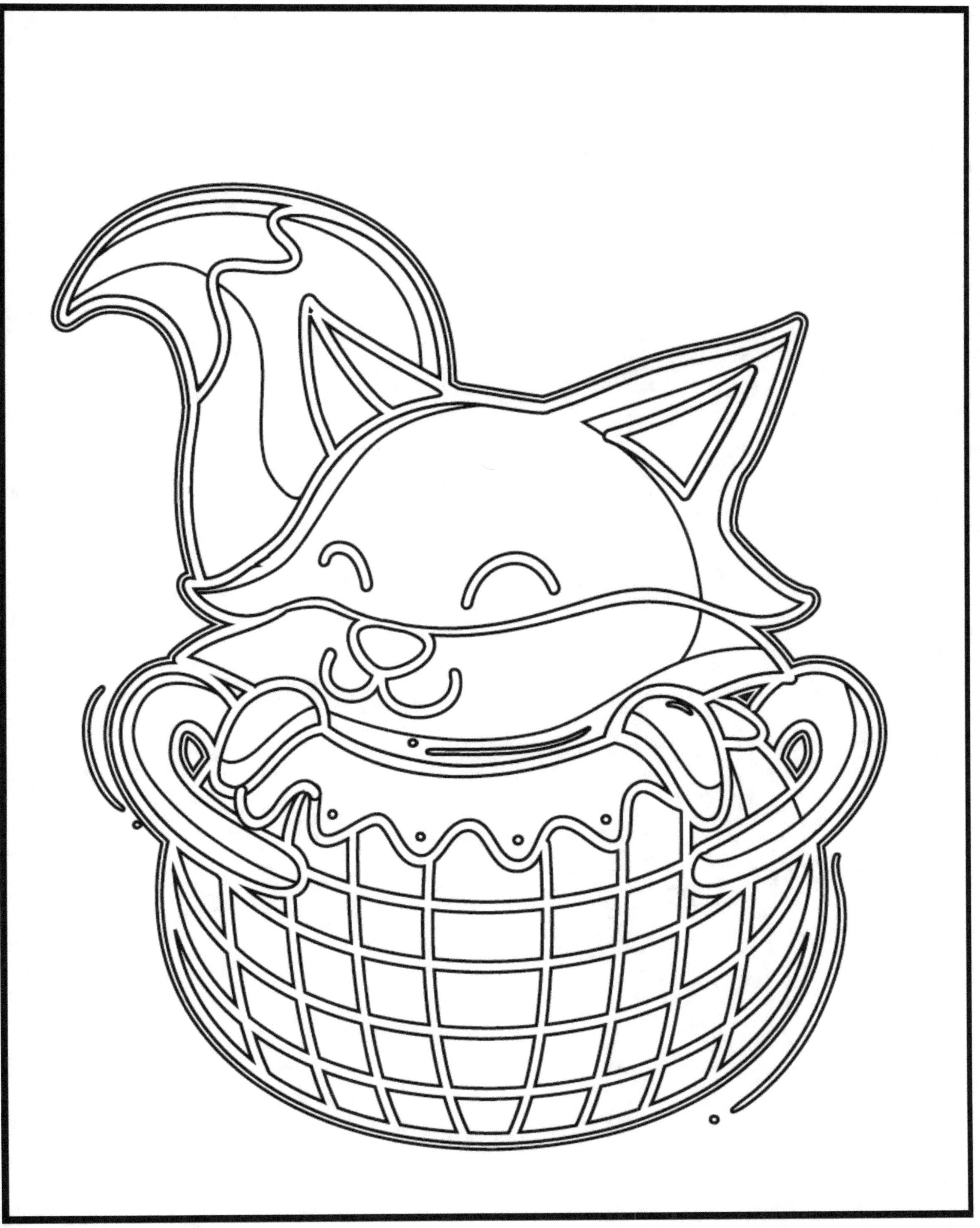